T0277545

MY CHILD IS TRANS, NOW WHAT?

MY CHILD IS TRANS, NOW WHAT?

A Joy-Centered Approach to Support

Ben V. Greene

ROWMAN & LITTLEFIELD
Lanham • Boulder • New York • London

Published by Rowman & Littlefield
An imprint of The Rowman & Littlefield Publishing Group, Inc.
4501 Forbes Boulevard, Suite 200, Lanham, Maryland 20706
www.rowman.com

86-90 Paul Street, London EC2A 4NE

Distributed by NATIONAL BOOK NETWORK

British Library Cataloguing in Publication Information Available

Library of Congress Cataloging-in-Publication Data

Names: Greene, Benjamin, 1999- author.
Title: My child is trans, now what? : a joy-centered approach to support / Ben V. Greene.
Description: Lanham : Rowman & Littlefield, [2024] | Includes bibliographical references and index.
Identifiers: LCCN 2023040342 (print) | LCCN 2023040343 (ebook) | ISBN 9781538186459 (cloth) | ISBN 9781538186466 (ebook)
Subjects: LCSH: Parents of transgender children. | Transgender children. | Parenting.
Classification: LCC HQ759.9147 G74 2024 (print) | LCC HQ759.9147 (ebook) | DDC 306.874086/7--dc23/eng/20231017
LC record available at https://lccn.loc.gov/2023040342
LC ebook record available at https://lccn.loc.gov/2023040343

To little Ben in 2015:
Thank you for choosing to stay so I could write this book for you.

CONTENTS

INTRODUCTION

Welcome! Thank you for picking up my book. I'm thrilled that you have decided you want to begin (or continue) your allyship journey and that you've chosen me as your guide on that path. You're going to learn quite a bit about me as you go through this book, including parts of my own story of living proudly as a transgender man for the last decade. My hope is that within these stories you'll have moments where the window into my life becomes a mirror, showing you the stories of yourself, your family, your child, or whoever else you had in mind when you sought out this guide. In those moments, and throughout this book, I want you to imagine me not as Ben the Author, but as a ghostwriter for trans youth around the world.

To make language a bit simpler, I will be using the words "trans" and "transgender" as umbrella terms for people who do not identify with the sex they were assigned at birth, which includes nonbinary and gender expansive people as well. (Don't worry if these words or concepts are new to you; we'll go through some definitions soon.) It should go without saying that transgender people are not a monolith, and nothing I say will apply to every single trans person, but this is a great place to start your learning and build a foundation.

To begin, I want to share a few key pieces of my educational philosophy.

First: I don't care where you're starting from; I just care that you're starting. I'm not here to judge you or make assumptions about what you do or don't know already; I'm just here to teach. I acknowledge that different people are at very different stages of their learning journeys, so for each new topic or vocabulary word I introduce, there will be a short definition in the text. If you'd like a longer definition, there's an in-depth glossary at the back of the book. Feel free to jump back and forth as needed. You can also read the whole glossary first if you feel that would help you.

Second: Every conversation I have about the trans community has joy at its core; that's why I included it in the subtitle of this book! There are so many reasons that coming out is joyful. Not only has someone realized something profound and beautiful about themselves, but they have identified *you* as someone who is safe enough and important enough to share their truth with. That is worth celebrating! Focusing on the joy as you go through this journey is crucial, and this book is grounded in trans joy and celebration. Though many of these pages are filled with suggestions for solving problems that may arise, it is important to remember that **coming out and transitioning are not problems to be solved; the problem to be solved is *society's* response to coming out and transitioning.** Together we'll talk through how to prevent and deal with these problems as well as explore who or what specifically brought you here.

Third: They say, "It takes a village to raise a child," and I'd like to apply that saying to creating support systems for trans youth. There are so many people who are collaborators in the quest to build a better world, and whatever your role in the village, this book is addressed to you. Whether you're here for your child, your grandchild, your friend's child, your patient, your student, or just for trans youth around the world, you have an important role to play. Because it will get extremely hefty to refer to the person you might have had in mind when buying this as "The person you may or may not have bought this book for"—and even "TPYMOMNHBTBF" doesn't flow particularly well—I'd like to propose a different solution. In the spirit of making trans youth the center of this book and these conversations, I will be referring to the subject of this book as "your VIP," and you can fill in the blanks with "my child," "my patient," "my uncle's neighbor's cousin," or "trans youth in general" at will.

Fourth, and most importantly: I cannot possibly represent every trans experience. There are at least 3 million transgender people in the United States, and there is no possible way I can write anything that applies to all of us. Like any other group of people, no two trans people are alike, and I am sharing my story not as *the* trans experience, but as *a* trans experience. Foundational concepts and vocabulary may look the same, and there may be stories that hit close to home, but remember that at the end of the day every identity and experience is unique.

Seeing as we're going to be on this journey side by side, I would love to introduce myself. For the past four years, I have been working full time as a public speaker and LGBTQ+ inclusion advocate. I've spoken internationally for companies, conferences, hospitals, schools, nonprofits, and government organizations. I've taken trips to testify on behalf of trans youth at the Missouri state capitol and have spoken to countless parent support groups around the country. Most rewardingly, I have spent hundreds of hours on the phone with parents, grandparents, relatives, teachers, and friends of newly out transgender people, coaching them along their journey to become supportive champions for their VIPs.

The story of my career is certainly helpful in explaining how I gained the expertise to write this book, but that doesn't tell the whole story. If you want to understand *why* I'm writing this book, we'll need to go back a bit further.

When I came out, I was fifteen years old, and I was one of only two openly transgender people in my hometown (that I knew of). I was also one of the first transgender students at my high school. I came out during a health class presentation by sharing an analogy I created that defines being transgender as like sitting in a chair, which I'll share with you soon. After presenting that content to my peers, I closed the presentation by saying, for the first time, "I know all this because *I* am transgender, and my name is Ben." The reaction was generally very positive, and though most of my peers didn't understand my identity at first, they cared about me as a person and were excited to learn. I'm a very extroverted person, which means I loved all the opportunities I had to answer people's questions—but my role as an educator quickly grew beyond anything I could have imagined.

Because our health classes lacked transgender education, my health teacher added my presentation to the curriculum and brought me in the next year to teach the sophomore students about what it means to be transgender.

Through these classes, I learned how much I loved public speaking. Because our guidance staff lacked training on the trans community, I facilitated a workshop to help them better understand, respect, and affirm their trans students. Through this conversation, I learned that I had the ability to impact and inspire powerful people to make actual change. Because there were no older out trans students to look up to or learn from, all the students questioning their identities turned to me for guidance on how to discover their identities and share them with the world. Through helping dozens of students embrace their LGBTQ+ identities, I built and found a community around me and learned the many nuances involved with discussions of identity.

Reading that paragraph through a positive lens, it sounds like my high school experience was incredibly impactful: I found my life calling in public speaking, learned to be an advocate and a resource, and grew into my current personality as a "trans older brother" to much of the queer community at my school.

Reading that paragraph through a negative lens, it sounds like my high school experience was awful: There was no education for myself or my peers about my community, there were no mental health professionals who had a full understanding of transgender students, and there was no one I could look up to for wisdom or inspiration.

The truth of my experience lies somewhere in between. Needing to create every resource I wished I'd had was exhausting, but it also fueled my passion for education and advocacy. If I could go back in time, do I wish I hadn't advocated for myself? Of course not. But do I wish I hadn't *needed* to advocate for myself? Absolutely. When I first heard the phrase "be who you needed when you were younger," it immediately resonated with me, and that continues to be one of my guiding philosophies. The work I do as an advocate and an educator is all with the goal of creating supportive systems and resources so that the trans people who come after me don't have to. All my life I've been described as empowered, bold, and *brave*—and it's meant as a compliment—but I don't want to be those things. To put it more clearly, I don't want to have needed to be those things. I especially don't want *kids* to have to be those things. Kids should be joyful and curious, not courageous and strong.

I am writing this book for trans youth; even though they are not my intended audience, they are my motivators. I am writing this so that with your help, we can create a better world where trans kids can just be kids, where trans people have access to resources they need without having to build them first, and where no one needs to be brave just to be who they are. Advocating for myself was rewarding in many ways, but the stakes were often high and the pressure was exhausting. At times I felt like I had been thrown to the wolves, and the only thing that would keep them at bay was an endless supply of patience, information, and vulnerability. As an adult and a professional educator, I've learned how to supply these things, but as a child I felt like I was a candle burning at both ends. In writing this book, my first goal is to take some of the load off the shoulders of the youth who came after me, at least for a little while. My second goal is to help you learn how to do the same so that these incredible youth can focus on being anything and everything but brave.

Enough about me (for now)—let's talk about you. Whatever your reason for being here, and whoever your VIP may be, I'm betting you're experiencing a range of emotions right now. Perhaps you're feeling nervous, confused, overwhelmed, excited, or some combination of these and other reactions. There's no one "correct" way to feel, and you are probably experiencing a mix of positive and negative thoughts and feelings. In the pages of this book, we'll walk through many of those feelings, talk about action steps for impactful allyship, and unpack the roots of current stigma in different settings. You'll find personal stories and joy-centering exercises woven throughout the chapters; we'll share a few tears and maybe (definitely) a few laughs as well.

If you're reading this, I'm guessing you fall into one of these four buckets:

1. Your VIP came out to you, and you want to be supportive but aren't sure what to do next.
2. Your VIP came out to you, you do not think you responded well, and you're hoping to learn how to make it better.
3. You suspect your VIP is about to come out to you.
4. You're just being proactive in learning how to be a good ally.

Whether you fit in one of them, all of them, or none of them, this is the book for you. Wherever you're starting from, I'm betting you're anxious to start implementing some brand-new allyship tips, so I'm going to close out our intro with a piece of advice that can help you improve your allyship right away.

I want to start you off with the biggest tip I have: Listen to your VIP. Listen empathetically, listen with action in mind, and listen often. So much of the global conversation around trans youth has the core message of "these youth do not know what they're doing, and the adults here have to make the decisions for them." Just like any other individuals, trans youth know themselves and their needs best. This doesn't mean you aren't allowed to ask questions or do research on your own, but it does mean that you need to *accept your VIP as the leading expert on themselves.* Their expertise doesn't come from years of graduate study—it comes from years of self-study, reflection, and research.

In working to acknowledge their expert status, lean in to listening empathetically. Take time to understand how they're feeling and why they're feeling it. One exercise you can try is to sit down and really try to put yourself in their shoes. Ask yourself: "If I woke up tomorrow morning in a body I knew wasn't mine, how would I feel? What would I do to fix that?" Try to take at least thirty to forty minutes to genuinely sit with those thoughts and see where they lead you; this may help you understand your VIP a little better. It is worth noting that there is a lot more to transness than just the "born in the wrong body" story that dominated the media of the early 2000s, which is why what's most important is to listen to the specific feelings of your VIP and empathize with those.

Taking that empathy into account, continue to listen with action in mind. By this, I don't mean listen to their concerns and feelings and figure out what you should "do about it." Listen to what your VIP is saying; they will tell you what they need from you (and if they don't, ask). They may need you to work a little harder on getting their name and pronouns right. They may need you to help them come out to someone. They may just want you to be a listening ear. Every VIP will need something different, and no two people are the same. Listen to your specific VIP and take what they say as seriously as if another adult were telling you what they need.

Though it's fantastic to keep empathy and action in mind, it's important to also remember that as people grow and change—especially young people, who evolve before our very eyes—their needs will grow and change as well. When I first came out, I was not comfortable advocating for myself and requested that my friends not correct others at school when they used the wrong pronouns for me. I also didn't want my parents sharing my identity with any of their friends. After a few months, I felt ready to ask my friends if they'd help me correct my peers. A few months after that, I asked my parents if they could help me come out to our extended family and broader community. Now, as an adult, I am comfortable advocating for myself and just need my friends and family to give me support on my occasional rough days. Rather than listening to my needs once and holding tight to them forever, the people who were most supportive of me checked in regularly to see how I was feeling and whether there was anything else they could do to be better allies.

This book will provide you with a toolbox of knowledge and strategies to help build supportive homes, classrooms, offices, and spaces for trans young people—and the most beautiful part of a toolbox is the infinite possibilities it implies. Only your VIP can give you the blueprint of what they'd like to build using those tools, or whether they'd like to use certain tools at all. There is no one way for someone to go on this journey, so listening and following your VIP's lead, providing them with whatever tools they need along the way, is your best bet.

On behalf of myself and your VIP, thank you for being here. Supportive allies make all the difference in the world for trans people of all ages, and it warms my heart to know that there are so many people who truly want to do right by my community and be the champion allies that trans youth need. I'm glad you're here, and I can't wait to go on this adventure together. Let's dive in.

I

THE COMING-OUT
PROCESS

1

COMING-OUT BASICS

What Does It Mean, and How Do You Respond?

Given that a "coming-out" conversation is likely what spurred your desire to read this book, it seems fitting to start with a crash course on showing up as an ally in the days, weeks, and months following your VIP's coming out to you. If I were delivering this chapter as a stand-alone presentation, I'd likely call it "Trans Allyship 101." I'm going to spend this chapter sharing some of my most immediate and most impactful strategies for supporting your VIP or any trans person that you might know or meet in the future.

Before we jump in to all the specifics, I think it's important that we make sure we're all on the same page about the language we use when we talk about the trans community. This section won't cover everything, and I'd encourage you to go to the glossary for any terms missing here that you'd like to see defined, but this is a great place to start (or be refreshed!). First, a quick run-down of some key words:

Sex: The biological categories (male, female, or intersex) into which humans and most other living things are divided based on their reproductive functions, hormone levels, chromosomes, and a variety of other features

Gender: Someone's internal sense of being male, female, or another identity

Gender Expression: How someone manifests their gender identity, whether it is through clothing, hairstyles, mannerisms, and the like; often classified as masculine or feminine

Now I'd like to briefly dive in to the chair analogy I mentioned in the introduction that explains what it means to be transgender or nonbinary. Imagine that when someone is born, they're born sitting in one of two types of chairs: either a firm, tall stool or a soft, squishy armchair. This chair represents someone's biological sex. Most people are comfortable in their chair and are happy to stay there for all time. They identify as cisgender. Whether or not you know it, you probably identify as cisgender!

Cisgender: Having a gender identity that is the same as your sex assigned at birth

Sometimes, people feel uncomfortable in the chair they're sitting in. We've all sat in a chair before that doesn't feel quite right for whatever reason, and when that happens you are really aware of how much it doesn't fit. This feeling is called gender dysphoria.

Gender Dysphoria: A feeling of discomfort or distress due to a mismatch between someone's biological sex and their gender identity

For a while, when we as a society talked about trans people, it was exclusively through the lens of dysphoria and misery. Conversations about dysphoria focus on how we get from a −10 to a 0, which is great, but I also want to feel more than just neutral in my body. I want to feel joyful!

Gender Euphoria: A feeling of joy and comfort when someone's gender expression is aligned with their identity

People may go through all manner of changes in their journey, some to avoid dysphoria and others to find euphoria. Most are going to be a combination of the two. So when you're sitting in a chair that doesn't feel right, what's the easiest solution? Just get up and move to a different, more comfortable chair!

Transgender: Having a gender identity that is different than your sex assigned at birth

There are many ways someone may move to another chair, and we will take a deep dive into those throughout the book, but the key point here is that there is no one right or wrong way for someone to switch chairs; all that matters is that they feel comfortable where they're sitting. The other crucial thing to note here is that getting out of one chair and sitting down in another doesn't change who you are. I am still the same person I was when I was sitting on a stool; I'm just more comfortable in this armchair. There are things that may change, but the person that you know and love is still very much alive—they're just more comfortable.

This explains the most binary of identities, but there are also many ways people can identify outside of male and female.

Nonbinary: Someone who does not identify as exclusively male or exclusively female

Nonbinary is an umbrella term for any identity outside of the male-female binary, and there are a lot of identities under this umbrella, many of which are explained in the glossary. An important thing to remember is that nonbinary is not always the same as androgynous or genderless, and rejecting the gender binary doesn't necessarily mean someone rejects all things tied to masculinity and femininity.

There are many other terms that we'll go over throughout the book, but if you're hoping for a deeper dive right now, feel free to jump to the glossary. One thing I want to highlight is that people often tell me they feel overwhelmed or annoyed by the number of different identities and labels that exist, and they don't know how they're supposed to remember every identity out there. I'll let you in on a little secret—I'm a professional transgender person who spends all day talking about different gender identities, and I'll never know every identity that exists—and that's totally okay with me. What I *do* know are the identities of all the people in my life who matter to me, so if someone shares a new identity with me, I look for opportunities to learn more about that identity on my own and then find opportunities to ask my VIPs more about their experience of that identity.

All this is to say that rather than busting out your flash cards and making sure you're memorizing all the new labels, just prepare yourself for the possibility—and the probability—that you're going to meet someone with an identity that you haven't heard of before.

COMING-OUT BASICS

At this point, you've probably heard the term "coming out"—if not from someone in your life, you've read it at least once before this page. The act of coming out, to put it simply, is when any LGBTQ+ person tells another person about their identity. One of the most universal experiences of LGBTQ+ people is coming to the realization that coming out is an endless process. Because our society is structured with straight as the assumed default sexuality and cisgender as the assumed default gender identity, many LGBTQ+ people feel like they spend their whole lives coming out to others. As a "professional transgender person," I am as open about my identity as I possibly could be, and I still need to come out on a weekly basis to people who are meeting me for the first time.

As simple as it might sound, coming out can be one of the hardest, scariest things for an LGBTQ+ person to do. Even if you aren't a member of the community, you have probably experienced a coming-out moment yourself. If you've ever needed to share a deep, dark secret or be the bearer of bad news, try to remember how that felt. Even though coming out as LGBTQ+ isn't bearing bad news, the fear of a negative reaction is very similar. There's a terror that coming out will change how someone sees you, how they treat you, or even whether they want you in their life. Historically, a massive proportion of LGBTQ+ people, especially young people, have been kicked out of their homes after coming out. According to a study by Chapin Hall at the University of Chicago, although LGBTQ+ youth make up only 7 percent of the general youth population, they comprise 40 percent of youth experiencing homelessness.[1] Even if someone has no reason to think their family would kick them out if they came out, whether they've expressed a calm indifference or even outright support for the abstract LGBTQ+ community, there is a fear that their opinions might change when it's their own child or friend coming out. Regardless of the actual proportion of "good" to "bad" reactions to coming out, because worst-case-scenario stories are the type of queer story that are most dominant in the news and in mainstream media, they're the stories we come to expect. To drive this home, I want you to think for a moment about a TV show like the popular medical show *Grey's Anatomy*. If every episode featured a patient who came to the hospital for surgery but tragically died at the end, you likely wouldn't be too keen on going in for surgery even if you knew you had a world-renowned surgeon. For LGBTQ+ folks, seeing and hearing only terrible stories means expecting only terrible stories too.

For trans people, coming out happens in two "directions," so to speak. The first direction is when someone comes out to a friend or family member who knew them as the gender they were assigned at birth. When I came out in the first direction, I told my parents, family members, and close friends that I identified as transgender. I asked them to start calling me Ben and to refer to me using he/him pronouns, and I let them know that I would be changing the way I was living and presenting my gender from then on. It's important to note that my specific story isn't the only way to come out; not everyone chooses to change their name, their pronouns, or their presentation, but most trans people will have some type of coming out in this first direction, whatever form that may take. This is how someone comes out to their family, their childhood friends, the people at their high school reunion—anyone who knew them before they transitioned. The second direction is coming out to people who previously had no idea someone transitioned, people they meet later in life who just assume they are cisgender. This includes people like new romantic partners, new friends, or new coworkers. As an example, when I went to college many of my peers assumed I had been assigned male at birth and was cisgender, and when I came out to them it took the form of my sharing the story of my transition.

Both types of coming out are terrifying, especially when you have no idea how the people you are telling are going to react. As we discussed previously, the TV shows we watch, the books we read, and the news we hear are all full of stories of people coming out and not receiving the best reactions. Because of how little representation there is for trans people, we don't always have opportunities to see ourselves reflected in positive ways and therefore can struggle to conceptualize a coming-out conversation going well. Why wouldn't we be terrified?

Though in theory, you'd think it would be easier to come out in the second direction because you aren't asking anyone to change anything about the way they refer to or think about you, the unfortunate reality is that people can lose friendships, relationships, and jobs after sharing this part of their identity. One of the most common reactions—stated explicitly or otherwise—is that some people feel like they've been tricked or deceived, that the person coming out to them has been dishonest for not disclosing their identity immediately. An important reminder to share with folks who have this type of reaction is that trans and nonbinary identities are no different than other pieces of information from our personal (or medical) histories. Just as someone isn't entitled to know how many siblings I have, where I'm from, or my other personal stories and struggles, they aren't entitled to know about the history of my name or what medical procedures I've had in the past.

You may also hear the phrase "coming out to myself." This refers to when someone realizes their own identity and accepts it for the first time. In the next chapter, we'll do a deep dive on how to be supportive during the self-discovery process. I came out to myself as transgender in October of my junior year of high school. It took me a long time to fully understand and accept my transgender identity, and even longer to be able to say the words out loud. I first started questioning my gender months before coming out, but I tried finding other ways to explain the feeling and avoid what I knew, deep down, was true. Maybe I was just having weird, late puberty. Maybe I was just a really butch lesbian. (By the way, although neither of these was true for me, they can be true for others. It is possible and common, for example, to be a butch lesbian and not be trans. We'll discuss this topic at length in the section in chapter 2 around analyzing your assumptions, but for now it's enough to understand that expression is not the same as identity.)

Some people eventually choose to stop coming out. This is referred to as being "stealth." When you're stealth, people only know you as the gender you identify as. They have no idea that you ever identified or were perceived as anything else. There are a lot of reasons that people may choose to be stealth. Some do it because they don't want to be treated any differently because of their past. Some do it because they fear for their safety or job/ housing security. Others do it because coming out can be draining and they just don't want to keep doing it. Being stealth is a completely valid choice that's exclusively up to the individual.

RESPONDING TO COMING OUT

If your VIP has come out to you, take a moment to recognize how incredible that is. Coming out is often deeply terrifying, and despite all that fear, your VIP has decided they want to come out to you. They have decided that you are important enough and trustworthy enough that they can share this vulnerable piece of themselves with you, and there are a couple of crucial things you can do to help show them that they were right to trust you.

The first and most important thing is to acknowledge that it's okay if you don't have a perfect understanding of what their identity means right away. Many people go into coming out prepared with answers to common questions or resources to share. They may not need your immediate understanding, but they do need your immediate support. The nervousness of coming out doesn't end after saying, "I'm trans." The nervousness ends when you say, "Great! I support you. I'm here for you. I still love you." You don't need to understand anything to be able to say that, however they identify, you don't hate them for it. Being able to respond with love, whether it's in the moment or any time after, is crucial.

From here, your action steps are going to be much more specific to your VIP, but I want to go over some of the general things you should keep in mind. The first is addressing any questions you have about this new information you've received. I can understand having a lot of questions you may want to talk about right away. Whether or not you should ask them is a perfect time to practice "reading the room." How has the conversation gone so far? Is either of you seeming/feeling overwhelmed? Has it been particularly emotional? If you rush to bring up every question and concern you have, it may end up adding more stress to both parties. To the person coming out, it may feel to them like you are doubting them or their identity. To you, especially during the very first conversation about it, the questions could keep building off each other, causing you to spiral into a hole of nervous hypotheticals.

Some people go into a coming-out conversation with a rehearsed speech and a list of resources, prepared to answer all your questions. Others may not feel the need or desire to prepare as much, operating under the assumption that if you have questions, you'll do your own research. Sometimes people get thrown into situations where they must come out—ready or not—and have to come up with what to say on the spot. All of these are valid ways to come out, and for different people, different strategies make them feel the most comfortable. If someone has prepared resources, they'll offer them up to you. If they don't, you can ask them if they have any resources they could send you for you to do more learning on your own. If you want to ask them questions, check in with them first to make sure that they have the emotional energy to be teaching you in that moment.

That said, don't avoid questions entirely. Many of the trans youth I've spoken to have shared that they had parents who didn't ask anything, which gave the impression that they were okay with their child's identity but didn't want to know anything about them. This is reminiscent of the common anti-LGBTQ+ phrase "You can do whatever you want in private, but I don't want to have to see it in public," often tossed around in reference to LGBTQ+ people holding hands, showing affection, or generally being themselves in public. You likely aren't trying to send that message, but you also don't want to overwhelm them, so the best thing to do is find a balance of asking questions when your VIP is open to it and respecting their space when they aren't.

The good news is that you're reading this, which means you're doing something really powerful: You're finding resources outside of your VIP. Why is this so important? For some people, educating others about LGBTQ+ identities is enjoyable. Some people (like me) even teach others to be more supportive as their job. For others, educating people is exhausting, especially when there are so many easily accessible resources that answer many common questions. The message that sometimes comes across when a trans person is asked something like "What does trans mean?" is "This doesn't matter enough for me to put time into researching and reading about this, but I would like you to do that work for me and summarize it with no preparation." This is very likely not what people mean when they ask these questions; of course they mean well. But by doing independent research first and then asking questions about this research, the message changes to "I care, and I'm still curious and would love to hear about your specific experiences. I'm asking *you* these questions, not just asking the first trans person I happened to find."

As time goes on, you can have more conversations where you're asking questions or talking about what this person's transition is going to look like, but you don't need to pack it all into one lunch, one car ride, or one text conversation.

Throughout these pages, I'll be sprinkling in "joy exercises" to help continue to ground us in joy and celebration and find moments of love and happiness in this exciting time. As luck should have it, you've arrived at the very first of these exercises.

JOY EXERCISE: CELEBRATE COMING OUT

It's so crucial to remember that something incredible is happening. Your VIP feels ready to share their true and authentic self with the world, and they want you to be a part of that journey. There is often a lot of stress in the days/weeks/months leading up to a coming-out conversation, and now that you're past that initial conversation, it's a great time to celebrate. It doesn't need to be a huge party; there are so many kind little things you could do to celebrate or show your VIP that you support them and you're there for them. Ideas for celebrations (which vary based on your relationship to your VIP) include:

1. Baking/buying a cake with rainbow icing
2. Buying a pride flag for your VIP to hang in their room or in a home space
3. Having a small celebration with a group of trusted individuals (Ideas for a more extravagant celebration are coming up in chapter 4!)
4. Having a family photoshoot with your VIP presenting how they want to be seen to replace photos they may be uncomfortable looking at
5. Taking your VIP to their first nail salon, to get a gender-affirming haircut, or the store to purchase affirming clothes
6. Having a fashion show of their new, affirming clothes
7. Attending a pride parade
8. Watching a TV show or reading a book together that includes a positive representation of their identity

FAQ: NOW THAT MY VIP HAS COME OUT, DOES THIS MEAN I CAN SHARE FREELY ABOUT THEIR IDENTITY AND TRANSITION?

Great question. The answer, which you'll continue to find is a repeated refrain throughout these pages, is sometimes. It depends entirely on the person and can evolve over time. What you want to avoid is a situation referred to as "outing," meaning disclosing another person's LGBTQ+ identity to others *without their explicit consent*.

Outing can be extremely painful and upsetting, especially for young people who already feel like many parts of their transition process are outside their control. When I was first coming out, I would spend days or even weeks at a time preparing to come out to a specific person—anticipating their reaction and deciding what to say to them and when to say it. When someone shared my identity with that person before I was ready, those plans would rapidly spin out of control. I couldn't make sure they were told in a way that would ensure their support, and I couldn't be ready for their reaction. It was terrifying and upsetting for so many reasons.

When my parents first sat me down and asked if I'd like them to share the news with our family, family friends, and neighbors, they were met with an emphatic no. I was not ready for them to find out and didn't want my story to grow beyond my control. After a few months of living openly as Ben with my friends, my answer changed. I let my parents know that I was comfortable with them telling the people who knew me well so that the next time I saw them they would know to use the correct name. Even still, I didn't want them bringing it up to people they knew that had no specific reason to know. Since then, we've had updated conversations and they know they can share my story with anyone they think might benefit from hearing it.

I want to point out that these changes in my opinion weren't because I had realized I was wrong; my needs were specific to how comfortable I was at that moment in time, and they changed as I matured, received more support, and built more confidence in my identity. The most important way to know what your VIP is and isn't comfortable with is to ask, ask again, and then ask again next week.

PRONOUNS

Often (but not always) when people come out as trans, they'll change their name and their pronouns. Pronouns in particular have been a hot-button issue for a few years now, and I want to dispel some of the myths and misconceptions around them. I often have people say to me, "If you want to have pronouns, that's fine, but it's not for me." Transgender and nonbinary people did not invent pronouns; we simply normalized the practice of *sharing* our pronouns in new interactions. If I could call you he, or she, or they, then you have pronouns! Put very simply, a pronoun is just what we call ourselves and each other when we are not using our names. Words like *I*, *me*, and *we* are also pronouns. There are lots of reasons why trans folks share their pronouns in conversations: They want to be referred to correctly, they want to let others know they can share their own in response, and they want to establish their safety and allyship to the people around them, to name a few.

It's not just trans folks who benefit from normalizing sharing pronouns; there are lots of people with gender-neutral names or who don't fit neatly into visible gender buckets, and they deserve to be referred to correctly. For example, at one of my speaking engagements a few years ago I was sharing about why pronoun sharing makes a difference for me, and a woman named Alex chimed in. She said, "I work in sales, and predominantly over email. Everyone assumed I was a man for years, but now that it's more normal to share our pronouns I can do that and people will refer to me correctly!" This small, inclusive act can make a big difference for many people.

Preferred Pronouns

Historically, people referred to the pronouns of trans people as "preferred" pronouns, but the general community is looking to eliminate the use of the unnecessary adjective. Why? Because it implies that my pronouns are a preference, something that would be nice if people used when they felt like it, rather than a fact. To use another analogy, suppose you're ordering a pizza and when you go to set up the delivery, you're asked for your "preferred address." I know for me this would feel rather unnerving. Even though it probably means the same thing as just asking for your address, it leaves room for you to wonder if that pizza is going to actually show up at your house and not the house around the corner. It's a simple change that makes no difference for the people saying it but may make a substantial difference in the comfort of the person you're talking to.

The Singular They

Sometimes people will use pronouns other than he or she. The most common pronoun after these is the singular they, which has been met with a fair amount of controversy in some spaces. To eliminate any confusion right off the bat, here are my responses to the most common concerns people bring up about the use of they/them:

- "It's not grammatically correct."
  According to whom? Any search will find the singular they abounds and is considered acceptable by major style guides like the MLA, Chicago, and Associated Press as well as respected dictionaries like *Merriam-Webster*.
- "You can't just change grammar."
  Starting when? The first dictionary was written in 1604 and had 3,000 words in it, while the 2019 *Oxford English Dictionary* had 171,476 words in it. Clearly you can just change language. Historically speaking, language and grammar are far more flexible than we think, and the rules of language and grammar are frequently changing to reflect the way we use them.
- "But it's so awkward/clunky/weird; I haven't used it like that before."
  Once again, this is not quite true. Consider a situation where you're in a café and you see a notebook on a table. Would you pick it up and announce, "Hey, someone left his or her notebook on the table. If you recognize this and know him or her, please let him or her know I've got it." No, you wouldn't, because you would certainly sound awkward/clunky/weird. You'd probably say, "Hey, someone left their notebook on a table. If you recognize this and know them, please let them know I've got it." Why do you say "they" in this situation? Because you haven't seen the person. You don't know what they look like or how they identify because you have no idea who it is. There's no reason it

COMING-OUT BASICS

needs to be any more difficult just because you've seen what the person looks like. You're already a pro.

That said, it might still feel like a new muscle for you, and that's okay. What I suggest to folks, and what I actually did when *I* learned about the singular they for the first time, was the following: Take a trip to a local park, walk around, and use they/them pronouns on every squirrel that you see: "That squirrel, they're so cute. Look at them climbing that tree. I hope they get that acorn. Their tail is so bushy. Oh no—they fell out of the tree!"

Not only is this an adorable exercise, but it creates a completely low-stakes environment to practice new vocabulary where if you mess up, no one gets hurt. The squirrel doesn't care, they just want their acorn. Waiting until you meet someone who uses they/them to practice using those pronouns is almost a guarantee that you'll make a mistake in a way that genuinely negatively impacts someone, so it's best to prepare those skills *before* you need them.

If you feel like you're still struggling with the grammar around the singular they, imagine your VIP has a tiny mouse in their pocket, and when you talk about them, you're talking about two entities acting as one unit: "Are they coming to dinner?" "Is that their jacket?" "I hope they're taking care of themselves."

Neopronouns

What about pronouns other than he, she, or they? In addition to these three dominant pronouns, people also use pronouns such as ze/zem, xe/xir, or many others. These are referred to as neopronouns, and while they're not the most common, you might run into them at some point on your allyship journey. There are a wide variety of reasons people use neopronouns, but in general, think of it simply as an additional way to be creative with gender expression. Pronouns are essentially gender-based nicknames we use instead of our names, and folks who have unique experiences of gender feel that neopronouns can be a great way to capture that.

There are many different neopronouns, and I don't know the exact grammar or pronunciation of every one. What I do know, though, is the grammar of the pronouns of the people I meet and talk to. When I meet someone who uses pronouns that are new to me, I do whatever I need to at that moment to learn and remember those pronouns, which usually means asking, "If you don't mind sharing, what are the forms of those pronouns?" to make sure I'm getting the grammar right. If I'll be seeing that person again, I practice those pronouns when I'm alone because I want to be able to show respect for my new friend. Learn the pronouns of people in your life and be respectful and open when new people come into your life with new names, pronouns, and stories to share. It's okay if you feel like you have to ask a couple of times to make sure you get it right; the person you're talking to will see it as a sign that learning is important to you and that you care.

Using Multiple Pronouns

Sometimes a person will also use multiple different pronouns, most commonly he/they or she/they. There are many reasons someone might use multiple sets of pronouns, but in general it is because they are comfortable with both options. Whenever a friend shares with me that they're using multiple sets of pronouns, I like to ask how they like them to be used. Some people like to hear a mix of the two pronouns, while for others, it depends on how they're feeling that day or they context they're in (social settings versus professional settings, for example).

One thing I will note that I've heard from many folks who use multiple pronouns is that it can be frustrating when people "pick a favorite," usually the one that most closely aligns with their gender expression, and use that pronoun exclusively. While it might feel easy to decide that someone "looks like a she," practicing using a variety of pronouns for people regardless of their expression is a great way to break down some of our old habits and assumptions about how someone needs to look.

Assuming Pronouns

As more people are finding freedom in expressing their gender in ways that are outside of the norm, it's becoming less appropriate and less accurate to look at someone and try to guess their gender and their pronouns. If someone tried to guess your name, you'd feel uncomfortable and perhaps a bit confused, so why are pronouns any different? Both your name and your pronouns are simple, central elements of your identity, and we all like to feel seen as we are. Having our pronouns used correctly feels validating and welcoming. Having them used incorrectly is hurtful and usually brings up the question "Do you really know me at all?" While we might be able to guess someone's pronouns correctly a good portion of the time, I know I'd rather default to asking and have a 100 percent accuracy rate (or, said differently, a 100 percent respect rate).

This is a good time to double down on another important fact: Pronouns and expression don't need to "line up." Someone who uses she/her doesn't need to wear traditionally feminine clothes or act a certain way to "deserve" those pronouns. Someone who uses they/them doesn't need to present as a genderless, blank being to "deserve" those pronouns. Some nonbinary people use he/him, some trans women use they/them—there are no rules about who can or can't be called what. A note: If this paragraph caused some friction for you, this is a great opportunity to reflect more about where you learned the rules about how people need to dress or what they need to be called. It's okay to acknowledge that this may be a new way of looking at the world, and as a part of that transition, take some time discovering what emotions this brings up for you and why.

Nice to Meet You, What Are Your Pronouns?

But Ben, you may ask, how will I know how to refer to people if I'm not allowed to make any assumptions?

How do you know anything about anyone? You just ask! In general, asking people their pronouns when you meet them is a great inclusive practice. I don't just ask, either; I take every opportunity I can to share my own pronouns, and I advise others to do the same. Why is it so important to share your own pronouns if it feels like they're obvious from looking at you? The easiest answer is what we just talked about: it isn't appropriate to assume anyone's gender, including your own. Avoiding making assumptions doesn't just apply to people who "look trans," because there is no way to do that. It applies to everyone. At this point in my transition, very few people I meet day to day know that I am transgender, and sometimes when I am singled out in a group to be asked my pronouns, I feel like I've just lost a game of transgender

"Where's Waldo." Not only does asking everyone their pronouns help build a more respectful environment, but it also helps build a safe one. Sharing your own pronouns lets the person you're talking to know that you are choosing to be an ally to the trans community. Whenever I meet someone and they share their pronouns or have them in their email signature or on their LinkedIn page, I imagine they're waving a teeny-tiny pride flag and saying, "I support you." In a larger group setting, someone sharing their pronouns identifies themselves as an "other" in the group if no one else shares. They have to choose between sharing their pronouns and identifying themselves as different from everyone else or skipping that conversation and risking being misgendered. Cisgender allies sharing their pronouns eliminates this internal debate and establishes a space where sharing your pronouns is perfectly normal. Share them when you meet someone, share them in your email signature, share them around a room when you hang out in a new group. Make sharing them as common and small a deal as sharing your name.

NEW NAMES

It's also common for people to change their names when transitioning. (Yes, this also means you might have to remember a new nickname for them if they had a nickname based on their name.) Figuring out a new name is one of the most exciting—and most challenging—parts of the journey of coming out. Many people go through quite a few ideas before settling on one name. Some—like me—will ask their parents, "What would you have named me if I were born a boy/girl?" Others go for a derivation of their birth name, while many look to favorite fictional characters or scour the internet for baby name registries to find something that feels just right. Trans people often refer to their original name as their birth name or their deadname. For many, but not all, trans people, hearing their birth name can be really upsetting, like a punch to the gut, a reminder that some people may never see us as we truly are. This is why some people use the term deadname—even though it may sound a bit dramatic, it properly communicates the weight of how hurtful it can feel to be called the wrong name. For others, it's no big deal. Some people get curious and ask trans people what their birth name was. This is a general no-no, especially if you've just met the person. If it's information they're comfortable sharing with you, either they'll bring it up or there will be an appropriate time to ask about it later. As curious as you may be, remind yourself that knowing someone's birth name isn't usually relevant to your conversation or relationship with them.

Storytelling and Old Names

This brings up a question that I've heard many times: If I want to tell a story about a trans person from before their transition, do I use the name and pronouns they used back then? Generally, I'm going to advise you to talk to the person you're wondering about with this question. Some people have no issue with you using their birth name, while others are uncomfortable with it. Some are fine if you use it around people who knew them before their transition (in storytelling contexts) but don't want anyone new to learn what it was. Ask your VIP how they feel about this. Perhaps you're wondering about this concept more broadly or aren't easily able to ask the person. Maybe you're wondering on behalf of someone like Caitlyn Jenner. In these cases, I would recommend that you default to using the name and pronouns they use now. The name or pronouns you use probably don't change the meaning of the story significantly, but intentionally misgendering someone is something you should try to avoid. Additionally, if you're talking to people who are still very early in their learning and support journey, they may misunderstand you and take your storytelling as a sign that you only need to use someone's correct name and pronouns when you feel like it. If you're feeling lost and wondering what to say instead to introduce a story like this, consider language like "Before John transitioned . . ."

Correcting Mistakes

So what should you do if you call someone the wrong name or the wrong pronouns by accident? The most common reaction I see when someone realizes they've referred to someone by an incorrect name is to panic. Let's imagine that Margaret's friend Britney recently came out as trans and now goes by John. Margaret has just referred to him as Britney in a casual conversation. She then says, "Oh gosh! I'm so sorry! I shouldn't have called you that, I'm a terrible ally! It's been so hard for me to remember; you know I've just known you for so long, but I'm getting there! I'm trying! I'm so sorry!" Maybe she even starts to tear up because she feels so awful.

At first glance, of course, Margaret's words seem kind. They're apologetic and explanatory and try to correct the mistake, and she likely genuinely feels bad about calling him the wrong name. Unfortunately, intention doesn't always line up with impact. Let's look at this situation from John's perspective. How might Margaret's words make him feel? What messages is she sending him? She's telling him that his name change is difficult and stressful for her and that he should feel bad for "putting her through this." Maybe she needs to be comforted because of how upset she is that she considers herself a "bad ally," and now John is in the position of having to comfort her instead of getting the comfort that he perhaps needs right now. This situation has been blown up, so it's at the forefront of everyone's minds—and the blame for the problem has been put on John for changing his name in the first place.

Though different people have different needs, the common consensus is that the best thing to do in this situation is correct yourself, apologize briefly, and move on in the conversation as fast as possible. If they need it, comfort the person, but the smaller a deal you make it to the other person, the less it will impact them. That being said, it will likely still have some kind of impact—it's never fun getting misgendered—and if the person needs some space, let them have it. In short, Margaret could have just said, "Sorry, John," and kept talking.

If you notice you're calling someone the wrong name or pronouns a lot, it's likely time for you to do some introspection. Have you put in the mental work to adjust how you see and think about this person? Do you use the correct pronouns and name in your head or in conversations when they aren't there? Repeated misgendering by a trusted friend or family member feels much more intentional, even if it isn't, and can be much more hurtful than a one-time slipup. Make sure you're using the correct pronouns in your head, and try to spend some time on your own practicing referring to them correctly. (The emphasis here on your own—if you practice by yourself, no one gets hurt when you mess up.) It's easiest for you to treat them the way they want to be treated if you see them the way they want to be seen. If you're still struggling to get them right, consider trying this trick: Every time you use the wrong name or pronouns, use the right ones in a sentence three times. This will help you adjust the way that you think about the person.

Talking about practicing pronouns gives us space for two important reminders. First, it's important to give yourself grace as you're learning someone's new pronouns. It's going to take you a moment to overcome some muscle memory, and that's okay. Second, acknowledging that it can be challenging and takes time also means acknowledging that it takes *effort*. The people in my life who I had the most patience with were not necessarily the individuals I knew it was "hardest" for; it was with the individuals who I knew were *trying* the hardest.

JOY EXERCISE: THE MISGENDERING JAR

This exercise is a fun one for helping remember your VIP's new name or pronouns. Set up a misgendering jar in your kitchen or another central location, where everyone puts a dollar any time they use the wrong name or pronouns. When it fills up, let your VIP use it for ice cream, a new video game, or anything else they want. Depending on how waterproof you are, you could also think about something like a "misgendering spray bottle." These might sound like silly recommendations, but they provide an easy avenue for your VIP to correct someone who uses the wrong pronouns, a helpful reminder with some gentle positive reinforcement, and as an added bonus they add some comic relief to what might otherwise be a challenging situation.

Correcting Others

What if you aren't the one making the mistake? What should you do if you hear someone else refer to a trans person with the wrong name or pronouns? Whether or not the trans person is there, it's a good idea to correct the person. If the person isn't there, you should speak up because if they'll say the wrong thing behind the person's back, there's a good chance they'll say it to their face too. But you may wonder: if the person is there, why should it be you? Unfortunately, not everyone is making as wonderful an effort as you, and may not take kindly to being corrected. Many times, when I've corrected others on my pronouns they've become upset, yelled at me, or even threatened me. Other times they've been kind but requested a significant amount of extra education in that moment that I haven't always had time to give. Because of this, the combination of the distress caused by misgendering and the amount of emotional energy required to correct people makes many trans people just stop trying.

Personally, if I don't correct someone it's not because I don't care or it doesn't upset me. I am upset, but I'm also exhausted. In high school, I had a friend who would correct everyone for me. Most often it was in gym class, and I was terrified to correct the other kids—especially the typical high school boys who you couldn't pay to respect each other, let alone a trans person. But this friend would get right up in their faces and say, "Nope. He." Every time. It took me a few years to fully understand how much of a difference that made for me. She made me feel safer and more like a man than the rest of the school did combined, especially when I first came out. When I reached out to others in the community to ask what advice they would share, the most common answer was to stand up for trans people whenever and however you can, and standing up when someone uses the wrong name or pronouns is one of the easiest and most impactful ways to do that. It doesn't need to be nearly as assertive as my high school friend was; it can be as simple as "I think she's actually going by Samantha now" or "I believe their pronouns are they/them." If you'd like to offer additional support, you could also say something like, "I know it was a little confusing for me at first too, but we can practice together if you'd like!" to help encourage them to practice learning your VIP's name or pronouns.

ASKING QUESTIONS

Humans are naturally curious, and the more different something or someone appears to be, the more questions we may have. There aren't many trans stories being told in most forms of media, so often when people meet trans people, their curiosity explodes and they have a lot of questions they want to go right to the source about. Many trans people feel like when they come out, they have to become a walking encyclopedia, whether they like it or not.

There are two main problems with this. One is that for each trans person who comes out, there could be a hundred people who decide to get educated and "go to the source." It can be exhausting giving vocabulary lessons and answering questions repeatedly, especially when there are more and more resources available that aim to answer those specific questions. By reading this book, you're doing exactly the right thing to help reduce that burden: You're seeking out those resources independently! There are thousands of trans people who run YouTube channels, write books, run blogs, post on Instagram and TikTok, and find other ways to share stories and information that you can use to get a basic understanding of what the trans community is. Of course, it's great to ask your specific friend about what their experience is, what their needs are, how they identify, and so on. In general, there's no harm in prefacing a question with, "Hey, do you mind if I ask a question about _____?" That way they can let you know if they have the energy to be in teacher mode, and if they aren't up for it, it's significantly less awkward than if you just ask them the question and they don't want to answer it.

A second and more substantial problem is that many people's curiosity tends to cross the boundaries of what is and isn't appropriate in normal conversation. Almost every trans person I know has at least one story of being asked by a complete stranger something along the lines of, "So . . . what genitals do you have?" or "What surgeries have you gotten?" As I'm sure you can imagine, it's horrifying to have someone you've never met asking one of the most private parts of you (so private that society has given them the nickname "private parts"). Though it would feel ridiculous to ask any cisgender stranger such specific questions about their genitals, many people feel that because trans people are so different, many of the rules about appropriate social conduct don't apply to them. It just makes us feel like misfits to be ogled at by the world around us.

One of the most common questions I get when I run trainings is, "What *can* I say? I have questions I want to ask, but I'm worried I'm going to offend someone!" A good litmus test I like to suggest is to imagine if the situation were reversed. Think about how close you are to the person—Are they a close friend? A coworker? A stranger?—and the place you currently are— Are you by yourselves? In the workplace? With a group of friends?—and think about how you would feel if that person asked you the question you want to ask them. If you feel like you'd be uncomfortable with them asking you, it's probably best to skip it. If you're still not 100 percent sure, ask a lead-in: "Hey, do you mind if I ask a question about ____?" This way, you can avoid embarrassing both of you by asking a potentially invasive or uncomfortable question.

Another question to ask yourself, especially if you're not your VIP's parent, is, "Do I want to ask this question because I am curious or because it will help me give this person the best care/support possible?" There are times where you may need to ask a personal question in a therapy context, or a medical context, or because it will help work out a challenge with a peer—but there are also times where these questions aren't relevant.

FAQ: WHAT CAN YOU DO IF YOU FEEL YOU'VE SAID THE WRONG THING?

As human beings, we're all bound to make mistakes and say or do things we wish we could go back and change. Whether this was a first coming-out conversation or a more specific situation, you may have said something that was harmful, whether you knew it or not.

There are different "levels" at which you might have done something wrong. Maybe you said one phrase or question that you can tell your VIP is upset about, but they're still a part of your life. Maybe your VIP isn't speaking to you or is living somewhere else and has cut off contact entirely. Maybe you were involved in anti-trans activism and are trying to do a one-eighty and learn to do better. Maybe you're being proactive and just want to know what to do if you do or say something wrong in the future.

Wherever you're starting from and whatever you've done in the past, I firmly believe there is always time and opportunity for you to grow, change, and contribute to building a kinder world. That said, it is also important for you to be accountable for any harm you may have caused, through both meaningful apologies and a commitment to making sure it doesn't happen again.

So how do you go about ensuring meaningful change? The first step is reflection. Take some time to either write, think, or talk through the following questions:

1. What did I say/do to hurt my VIP?
2. Do I understand why it was hurtful?

If you aren't sure of the answers and just have a general sense that your VIP is upset, I encourage you to reach out to your VIP to ask, if that is an option. Make sure they know that you're not trying to rehash that conversation; you want to learn so you can reflect and grow to make sure you don't say or do it again.

The second step is to unpack why you said or did what you did. Write, think, or talk through the following questions:

3. Did I know in the moment that this was going to be hurtful?
4. Why did I say/do that?
5. Was there a specific thought, feeling, or topic that caused me to say that? Is this connected to something I learned/experienced growing up?

These questions might take some time to think through, and that's okay. They can be great tools to start conversations with trusted partners, friends, therapists, or to spend a few days thinking about.

Lastly, it's time to think through the solution! Write, think, or talk through the following questions:

6. Do I still believe what I said/did?
7. How can I make sure I won't say/do that again?

If you answered yes to question 6, that's okay. Transphobia and homophobia are quietly yet profoundly baked into many of the structures, systems, and media we're exposed to every day, and it can take time to unlearn the harmful biases we've developed over a long period of time. One of the best ways to conquer bias is to learn more about the group you hold biases toward, as this usually contradicts biases or expectations, so reading this book can help!

Now that you've reflected critically, it's time to apologize. Unless your VIP asks otherwise, this apology shouldn't focus on explaining why you said what you did, as this may end up creating a situation that is just as upsetting as the one you're apologizing for. Rather, focus on making a genuine apology and sharing a brief window into what you're doing to make sure it doesn't happen again. Most importantly, remember that actions speak louder than words—prove that you have learned and grown by sticking to the changes you decided you would make and doing better moving forward.

At this point you may be thinking, "Gee, Ben, that sounds like a lot! Is there anything I can do to make sure I don't say anything hurtful in the first place?" The answer: no . . . and yes. I say no because we're all human beings, and even I (a trans person literally writing a book on trans inclusion) still make mistakes and am learning and growing all the time. I say yes because we can absolutely minimize the chance of those mistakes happening by being proactive about our learning. Unlearning our biases and understanding what makes a statement hurtful will help us move past harmful beliefs and avoid saying harmful things to our VIPs.

To dramatically oversimplify things for a moment, nearly everything trans people want in the realm of validation and psychological safety can be boiled down to two things:

1. I want to be seen and respected as I am, not as how people want me to be.
2. I want to be supported in achieving goals related and unrelated to my identity.

Almost all hurtful things someone can say or do fall into one of the two "anti-buckets" of those desires:

1. I do not see you as you are.
2. I do not support you in your transition, identity, or goals.

Even if you don't say one of those two phrases explicitly, you may have shared one of them as an underlying message. Here are a few examples of common harmful phrases and the message behind them that explains why they're hurtful:

- Using the wrong name/pronouns
  Message sent: I do not see you as the name and pronouns you use, only as who you used to be or who I expect you to be based on your appearance.
- "I don't support you cutting your hair/having surgery/coming out because I'm worried you'll regret it."
  Message sent: I do not see your identity as something that is true or long-term for you, and I do not support you.
- "I'm grieving my daughter/son."
  Message sent: Who I thought you were is more important to me than who you actually are; you are just your gender to me.

This is also a great place to highlight impact versus intent. Even if you did not *intend* to send a harmful message, the *impact* was hurtful, and it's important to acknowledge and own up to that. As we talked about earlier, with any mistake, owning up to and understanding the impact is a crucial step. As you walk through life sharing questions and concerns with your VIP, make sure you're considering not just your intent but also the impact your words might have on them.

Finally, if there is someone in your life who you think you've done a lot of harm to and you're on the road to healing, acknowledge that it may take time for that healing to occur. For trans people, we hear hurtful phrases like these all the time and are often told we're not allowed to be at all upset about it because people are learning. While it's true that people are learning, it also feels like death by a thousand paper cuts: The impact of one seemingly small mistake can feel far larger when piled on top of so many other experiences, small and large, that we have daily. Give people grace and space to process and heal on their own, continue your own growth and healing, and hopefully you will be able to find peace and love with each other again.

KEY TAKEAWAYS

I know the stakes likely feel high following the coming-out conversation you had or anticipate having. Indeed, the time following your VIP's coming out is a crucial window for making sure they know they're loved and supported, and there are two important reminders I will hammer home before closing out this chapter.

1. *It's okay if understanding comes on day 5, day 10, or day 100—as long as love and respect come on day 1.* You may not understand everything about your VIP's journey right away, and that is completely normal, but you don't *need* to understand every part of their identity to show up for them with love and compassion.

2. *All we can do is be better tomorrow than we were today.* As a human being, you're guaranteed to make mistakes. The big question isn't whether you will make mistakes, it's what you will *do* about those mistakes. Don't dwell on them or continue to beat yourself up; just try to be better tomorrow.

2

"COMING OUT TO MYSELF"

Supporting Your VIP through Questioning, Exploration, and Discovery

Whatever stage of their journey your VIP is in, a large part of that journey is going to consist of self-reflection, self-doubt, and self-exploration. Even now, almost ten years into my own transition, I find myself reflecting on new questions about my own experience of my gender identity and what that means to me.

Remember, self-reflection or identity questions don't always mean that someone is "no longer trans"—it simply means they're curious about their experience of their identity. While we explored the process of coming out to others in the last chapter, I want to take a step back and talk more about the process of gender curiosity and exploration.

I didn't have what some might consider the "classic trans experience": I didn't hate dresses or beg desperately to be allowed to play only with the boys. For a long time, I was a self-defined "weird girl." I wasn't particularly masculine; I just didn't fit very well with "normal girl things." I only wore patterned pants, didn't like makeup, and didn't have many close friends. I didn't have any words or thoughts beyond that; I just assumed I was weird or "bad at being a girl."

During my sophomore year of high school, I realized I identified as bisexual, which was quite easy to figure out. I had the vocabulary to describe a crush, and I knew that I had a crush on a good friend of mine. (While I plan to be very vulnerable in this book, I won't be sharing anything about this crush because she did not know about it, and I would like to keep it that way.) Because I knew there were other queer students at my school and had seen my friends react to queer folks before, I wasn't particularly concerned about their reactions. In the spring of that year, I began excitedly coming out to my friends as a bisexual woman.

One of the friends I told about my sexuality added me to a Facebook group specifically for LGBTQ+ youth across the state of Connecticut, and it was a revelation. Where before I had known countably few other queer people, now I was part of a group of hundreds of queer students just like me debating hot issues, sharing jokes, and even falling in love. Some of the people I met in that group are friends I'll have for the rest of my life. (One of them was even a best man at my wedding.) I finally felt seen in my queer identity.

In the summer following my sophomore year, as the effects of puberty became more pronounced, things became a bit less rosy. I started to feel uncomfortable in my body in ways I couldn't describe—I had moments where I'd look in the mirror for a long time: I would just stare into my eyes and lose the ability to recognize who was looking back at me. Sometimes I felt like I'd left my body altogether. I've since learned that what I was feeling was called dissociation, but at the time it just felt isolating and scary. What was particularly challenging about this feeling was that it wasn't like anything I had ever felt or heard described before. Not having language to explain what I was feeling meant I couldn't talk to friends, couldn't ask a guidance counselor, and couldn't research online.

Eventually, a member of the Facebook group posted that they were trans and how they had figured that out, and a lot of what was shared really resonated with me and ended up triggering an epiphany. Everything fell into focus, and suddenly there were so many words for how I was feeling. From there, I began sifting through a new kind of doubt: wondering if I was truly masculine enough to be a man. Most of my hobbies were seen as more feminine, I only had female friends, and I was (and still am) the least aggressive person I've ever met. I knew I wanted to be Ben, but I felt like I needed to "earn it," so for a number of months I became obsessed with becoming the perfect manly man. It came to a point where I would go to the mall with a friend who was also trans and we would sit in the food court and take notes on how all the men walked, how they held bags, and how they sat in chairs, then we would practice those movements and grade each other on how well we were performing manliness. Once I acknowledged that time for what it was—a performance—I had my second big epiphany: I could actually be a feminine man. There was no one who could tell me what kind of man I could be except for me. Once I gained confidence in that reality, my battles turned outward and, besides occasional and inevitable moments of doubt, I've stayed firm in that identity over the years.

Though realizing who I was gave me significant clarity, it was not all smooth sailing from there. I began to experience significant feelings of gender dysphoria, a feeling of discomfort or distress due to a mismatch between someone's gender identity and their biological sex. Everyone experiences dysphoria in a unique way, and not all trans people experience dysphoria at all, but for the remainder of my high school years dysphoria dominated my life. My dysphoria centered on my chest, and I couldn't go swimming or do any activity that required me to wear a T-shirt. I showered with the lights off, wore huge hoodies even in summer heat waves, constantly bound my chest (and ended up hurting my ribs quite a bit), and felt all-around awful pretty consistently.

In the decade since then, I've spent a lot of time reflecting on the ways things could have gone differently, and one of major points of pain for me is that I likely would have come out much earlier if I had known it was an option. Trans characters weren't in my books or on my TV shows. We didn't learn about gender dysphoria in my health class. I didn't have enough of a foundation to even know what to google to try to find support. This is sadly a very common experience shared by many trans people, especially those growing up in small towns: not having the words to describe dysphoria, not knowing there's a solution to that feeling for so many years, and then coming out very shortly after learning how to define how they're feeling. While some people mistakenly view learning the word "transgender" as the start of a journey or exploration, I have always seen it more as the final unlocking of a door that's usually full to bursting with questions, confusions, desires, and dreams. Thankfully, with increases in education and visibility, more people than ever are learning the words that align with their feelings and feeling more and more comfortable coming out when they're ready.

When I came out to my parents, they didn't quite get it at first—which of course I don't blame them for, since I was their first real exposure to the transgender community. They met me with love immediately—something I was immensely grateful for. The message they sent was, "We don't exactly understand yet, but we love you and we'll figure it out together." After the initial conversation, they processed in different ways: My mom spent hours doing research privately, working through her thoughts in her own way and coming to me periodically to ask about the things I was thinking about for my transition. My dad asked me questions frequently. Every weekend we went for a drive to get breakfast or to get our hair cut, and while we were in the car he would ask me about whatever had been on his mind that week. As time went on, they both grew in their knowledge and their support, and even though they were getting the information in very different ways, they both ended up in the same place: They understood me and supported me in all the ways I needed.

Just as I highlighted at the end of the last chapter, understanding can come on day 100 as long as love and respect come on day 1.

You may have noticed from my story that there was a bit of a gap between when I realized I was transgender and when I shared that information with my parents, and that in-between space was a hard place to be. If you believe your VIP is transgender or questioning their gender identity, there are a few things you can do to help them feel more comfortable, as well as a few things to avoid.

WHAT SHOULD YOU DO IF YOU *SUSPECT* YOUR VIP IS TRANSGENDER?

There may be a lot of reasons you suspect your VIP is transgender. Maybe they've started to dress or act differently, hang out with new people, or do other things that you've heard were "the signs" from the stories of others. Whatever the reasons, you are hoping to be proactive in your support, which is great! While it can feel tempting to jump straight into action or sending clear messages of support, I am going encourage you to pump the brakes for a moment and reflect more on what you've seen and heard so far.

Understanding Your Suspicions and Addressing Your Biases

First off, let me say that short of your VIP saying, "I am transgender," there is no sign that definitively means they are transgender. Though gender identity is innate, gender expression and the way that we are told to present our gender are learned. If a woman cuts her hair or starts to dress more masculine, or a little boy wants to play with a Barbie doll, this does not necessarily mean their identity has changed. Though they could be making a conscious choice to reject their assigned gender roles, it could also just be doing something that they felt like doing, with no larger implications. Whatever it is that your VIP is doing, consider *why* it makes you suspect they might be trans.

The reason breaking some of the gender-related "rules" we have in our society can seem so stressful is that we have been living within and enforcing those rules on ourselves and others for our entire lives. The younger someone is, the less time they've spent having those rules reiterated to them, which makes them much easier to break, intentionally or otherwise. This is why it is so common for younger children to want to say or do things that break those norms: They are just looking to do things that make them happy, and those rules aren't on their mind at all.

This is not to discredit trans experiences; many trans people experiment with things outside of their own gender role to see if it makes them feel more comfortable, and it often does! If someone wants to paint their nails or wear a suit to the prom, we shouldn't jump right to assuming they're trans, nor should we assure ourselves they aren't. If there are many, many of these instances over time, that is a bit more of a sign.

The biggest sign is if the person you're thinking about has been showing signs of gender dysphoria. Have they seemed frustrated, distressed, or unhappy about things related to their gender—perhaps putting up significant resistance to wearing dresses or pants or insisting that they be called a different name or pronouns? If you start to see this in your VIP, it might be helpful to offer them some small changes without any larger implications. Rather than asking them outright if they're transgender, ask simpler questions like: Would you like to try a new hairstyle? Would you like to get some different clothes? Is there something else you might like me to call you? It is important to note, however, that gender dysphoria is not a requirement to be trans. For some people, their gender assigned at birth just doesn't feel quite right, and they transition because it makes them happier. It's not all about avoiding dysphoria, it's also about finding euphoria.

The conversation about the role of gender roles (ha!) brings up a different question: Why do you want to figure out whether your VIP is transgender? Besides the obvious first answer—"Because I would like to have this information"—a second possible answer is, "So I know I should treat them differently (not worse, just different) based on their new identity." I'd like to encourage you to pause and think about how your relationship with and treatment of your child would change if they came out to you today. Would you suddenly suggest different activities or hobbies? Would you ask them different questions about what they want when they grow up? With all children, one of the best things to do is to meet them where they are and support their interests and passions, regardless of where those interests fall along gendered lines, and I encourage you to treat all your children with that sort of freedom from gender-based expectations. You may be surprised at how this freedom allows them to flourish regardless of their gender identity.

Understanding Coming-Out Timelines

At this point, you might be saying, "I have a lot of reasons to believe that my VIP is transgender and it feels like I'm doing everything right, so why hasn't my VIP come out to me yet?" Something that's really important to remember is that while comfort with you plays an important role in whether and when someone decides to come out, there are many other things at play in deciding to take that step. Coming out is *terrifying* for a lot of people, for a wide variety of reasons, many of which are internal. I came out over the course of a year, dragging it out for far longer than I needed to because of how afraid I was.

The biggest thing that made it hard for me to come out was that, most simply and most sadly, I didn't want to be trans. I was afraid, I had a lot of internalized biases against transgender people, and I knew that the road ahead of me would be a hard one. Even once I accepted it, saying the actual words out loud felt like a terrifying, impossible task. Just like any other difficult conversation, saying the actual words "We're breaking up," "I lost my job," "I'm sick," or "I'm transgender" is hard for reasons we can't always explain. This isn't because it's a bad thing, and coming out is not the same as dropping horrible news or breaking up with someone, but it does carry a similar weight because of how unpredictable the response often is.

The second thing I was afraid of was my parents' reaction—not because of anything they did or said, but because I had no model for a coming out that went well. Every TV show or book with a trans character that featured a coming-out scene usually ended with the trans character being kicked out of their home or not supported at all. It made for good drama, but as a young person who had never in my life heard a story of a coming out that went well, it meant that I simply assumed it would go badly because all coming outs went badly. I literally did not have the ability to imagine what it would look like for a coming out to go well because I had never heard of it happening. I had built up so much anxiety about what my parents' reaction was going to be that I spent hours coming up with the perfect responses to hundreds of different worst-case scenarios.

The third thing I was afraid of was coming out locking me in to one identity forever. I felt like I needed to know all the answers and have a full picture of my own identity before I could tell anyone else. I was also worried that if I ended up being wrong, or if my identity changed later on, people would be confused and I would have embarrassed myself. It's okay to have these fears—whether for yourself, your VIP, or someone else in your life—but it's important to recognize that this is a form of internalized transphobia. The way our social norms are set up, if you *really* "have to" deviate from the norm, it should be done as minimally as possible, coming out once and getting it over with so you can carry on business as usual. The reality is that we often spend years thinking, talking, and experimenting about everything else in our lives that is part of our identity: career interests, fashion style, even things like hobbies or favorite foods. Gender is another piece of our identity, so why should it be any different? It's okay for you to play around, be open, and maybe even get something wrong. We're all just trying to figure out who we are and where we fit in in this world.

Similarly, I was also afraid that coming out would lock me out of the safety of the closet. Once I came out, it made things real in a way they hadn't been before.

I tell you all this to help you ground yourself. If there is someone in your life who you know or suspect is trans, nonbinary, or a different identity in the LGBTQ+ community and they haven't told you, know that there is likely a lot going on that isn't about you. The best thing you can do is use every tool in your toolbox to show that you *will be* supportive whenever they're ready, however long it takes.

How to Show Subtle Support and Pass the "Litmus Test"

It is common among trans, nonbinary, and other LGBTQ+ people to try to find subtle ways to determine if someone is a safe ally. This usually involves trying to figure out if they have any close friends/family members in the LGBTQ+ community, if they watch any TV shows with positive representation, or if they admire any public figures with LGBTQ+ identities.

The first time I came out to my parents, it was as bisexual, which I was far less afraid to do. Why? Because my family watched an episode of *Modern Family* almost every night. We came together to watch Cam and Mitch, a comical yet authentic gay couple, and laugh not at their identities but at the funny situations they found themselves in. My parents had nothing bad to say about them, and it signaled to me that they were totally okay with gay people—and they were!

When it came time for me to come out as transgender, however, I didn't have as much of an "easy in" to bring it up around them. The main celebrity option that I could bring up without arousing suspicion was Caitlyn Jenner, who they made fun of at times. This stressed me out immensely because I assumed that they didn't like her because she was transgender. The reality—something that I realized about a year later—was simply that they didn't like what they saw and read about Caitlyn Jenner as a *person*, and their opinions about her were not reflective of their opinions about transgender people.

As a brief aside, this is an excellent opportunity to talk about language and allyship. Many people who consider themselves progressive allies like to misgender Caitlyn as a sign of intentional disrespect to show that they don't like her. Doing this, however, sends a message to transgender people that their respect of transgender identities is conditional to them liking you. I am *not* a Caitlyn Jenner fan, but that doesn't make her any less of a woman.

Ways to show your support or pass this test in advance include finding subtle ways to mention LGBTQ+ people you admire; watching a movie together with a trans protagonist; and making sure that if there's an LGBTQ+ person you don't like (which is allowed as long as it's not me), when you make comments about them you don't bring their identity into it. It's also worth noting that watching movies/TV shows with positive representations of LGBTQ+ people with your kids who you don't suspect might be trans is still a great idea, because it will help them build empathy and understanding for people with identities and experiences different from their own and will help them grow up to be inclusive, accepting humans!

WHAT IF YOU FIND OUT BEFORE YOUR VIP IS READY?

So far, we've been talking a lot about the act of intentionally coming out, which assumes an element of choice that unfortunately isn't always the case. If someone discloses the gender identity or sexuality of anyone without their consent, it's referred to as "outing" them. While in the last chapter we discussed how to avoid outing your VIP to others, what should you do if they're outed to you?

In general, a large part of the reason being outed is so upsetting is that it takes the whole situation out of their control. Whenever and however possible, we want to send a clear message that they are still in control. Your response in this situation depends on if they know that you know. If they don't know, even though it might be tempting to go right to them, it's best to leave it in their hands and wait for them to come to you. Directly asking them about it is likely to make the conversation feel more like a confrontation, and they will likely experience high levels of stress because they aren't prepared for it. If a significant amount of time has passed or you feel strongly that you'd like to talk to them about it, consider writing them a note/message or gifting them a token of support like a pride flag. This gives them the opportunity to process privately before coming to have a conversation with you about it.

The important thing is to focus on sending a clear message of support and letting them know they have control over the situation. As an example: "I saw the letter you got today addressed to Joe Schmo, and just wanted to let you know that I love and support you no matter what. I won't bring this up with anyone unless you tell me otherwise, and we can talk about this whenever you're ready. There is no rush, I'll be here whenever you want."

If they were present when you found out or they definitely know that you know, it's important to share a similar sentiment as quickly as possible, as they may view your avoidance of the topic as you hoping it isn't true or not wanting to support them.

It is crucial that you hold true to your words and don't share anything about their identity with others before they're ready. If they are open to it, have a conversation with them about what names and pronouns they use and how they'd like you to refer to them when you're alone together versus when you're around others. If you found out before they were ready, they're more likely to not want you sharing their chosen name with others.

As an important aside, you know yourself best, and some people find it easier than others to remember to use different names in different situations. It's okay if that is something that would be too challenging for you, and it's important to be honest and not create situations where you're more likely to use the wrong name or pronouns. You can also find ways to casually incorporate gender-neutral language or nicknames that are an alternative as a subtle show of support.

Remember, it's easy for your VIP to feel like everything is completely out of their hands, so anything you can do to help give them power over their story will help the situation feel much safer and more manageable.

EXPLORING TOGETHER

New Names

One of the most exciting, and occasionally most challenging, parts of the coming-out process is the selection of a new name. As I said in the last chapter, not every transgender or nonbinary person will change their name, but it is relatively common. Our names are a fundamental part of our identity, and not many people get the opportunity to name themselves in a way that reflects that identity, so it's important to make sure you follow your VIP's lead as they think through different ideas for their new name. Some folks know right away, while others try on different names for months before they find one that feels like home.

For me, I grew up as one of three girls, and we often asked our parents what they would have named us if we were born boys, and their answer every time was Benjamin. I chose Benjamin because it felt predestined and because

I thought if I gave them the son they'd planned for, they'd be more willing to accept me. For my middle name, I decided to pick something more personal and meaningful. Early in my transition, when my support system was limited to my best friend and my girlfriend, we would spend time together as our true selves and dance to the song "Riptide" by Vance Joy. That song became closely associated with those people, and I listened to it each time I felt alone to remind me that I had people who saw me as I was and loved me all the same. To pay homage to those people, and to the ways they got me through that difficult time, I picked the middle name Vance.

These two methods are very common in the list of strategies for picking new names. Other strategies include things like recalling a favorite historical or fictional character with a particularly cool name—I know quite a few Percys (after Percy Jackson) and Artemises (from Greek mythology)—or simply spending time browsing baby name websites. Once your VIP has a list of possibilities, you can find fun ways to "test run" those names together and see how they feel with your VIP. One of the most popular ways to try out new names is to visit a number of coffee shops and at each one give a different name to see how it feels when it's called out.

Learning a New Name

Now that your VIP has their new name and/or pronouns picked out, it's time to make a habit out of using them! I know it can feel challenging at first, especially if you've known your VIP for a long time, but over time it will become completely natural. What's important to highlight here is the difference between *memorizing* someone's name and pronouns and *learning* them.

When you memorize someone's name or pronouns, you may find yourself having thoughts like, "I have to remember that *he* wants to be called *she* now." This layer of mental gymnastics is only going to serve to thoroughly confuse you and make it far more likely that you'll use the wrong pronouns in front of your VIP. On the flip side, when you learn someone's pronouns, you have to actually change how you've conceptualized them.

I know this sounds like a confusing new skill, but it's something you've likely done before. Have you had a friend or family member get married and change their name? Most of us have, and though it took some time, we changed the way we conceptualized our married friends' names and understood that their new name is who they now are. Outside of names and identities, there are plenty of things that go into our conceptualization of a person that we often have to update. If your friend Bob leaves his job as an accountant to work at a pharmacy, he's not an accountant who works in a pharmacy, he's a pharmacist. We know that accounting is a part of his story and his history, but it isn't who he is anymore. Now take this lens and apply it to your VIP: Change your concept of them and their gender to be what they've shared with you, not what it used to be.

If you need a tactical way to practice this, find opportunities to practice on your own, like while folding laundry ("This is his shirt," "He wears these socks," etc.) or at a dinner with another supportive person having a conversation about your VIP. This second option is a great one to propose if you know there are other people in your VIP's circle that are struggling with names and pronouns.

As you're learning, it's understandable that mistakes may happen, and we discussed earlier in the book why mistakes can be so hurtful and what to do when you make a mistake, but the more efficiently you can work through your thoughts and become a name/pronouns pro, the less likely it is that you'll do any long-term damage to your relationship with your VIP. It's important to remember that being new on your journey isn't a Get Out of Jail Free card for saying things that have a hurtful impact, and you can't assume you will be automatically forgiven just because you're trying. Of course there should be grace in the process, but we should ground ourselves in remembering that this isn't just your independent journey; it is a journey with lasting impacts.

Wardrobe and Appearance Changes

In addition to changing names and pronouns, there are also some things about your VIP's appearance that may change. They may change things like their clothes or their hair, or they may not. This is an important time to remember again that gender identity and expression are not the same thing, and someone doesn't need to dress a certain way to "earn" their identity. That said, many people will change the way they dress as they learn more about who they are.

There are myriad ways you can help with or celebrate these changes:

- Help your VIP look at different hairstyles they'd like to try, or offer to join them on a trip to the barber/salon to get that hairstyle.
- If you or someone you know is comfortable with Photoshop, try photoshopping a recent picture of them with a few different hairstyles they're considering.
- Join them on a trip to the mall to try on new clothes that fit the style they're looking for.
- Put together a collection of pictures of people with a personal style that your VIP enjoys to help them figure out what new clothes they might want.

It's also worth noting that getting an entirely new wardrobe can be expensive, but it doesn't need to be! One of my favorite resources in the queer community is a clothing swap or community closet, where folks can donate clothes that don't affirm their identity or that they aren't going to wear anymore and trade them for clothes that make them feel more seen. This is a great way to help lots of people all at once find new affirming clothing without breaking the bank.

Finding the Right Label

Sometimes it takes a moment for people to figure out what label works best for them, which can be stressful both for your VIP and for you and others around them. Maybe they are fluctuating between different names or pronouns. Maybe it feels like they have a different identity every day. This part of the process is very normal, and typically people will fluctuate and explore until they find something that feels like home. As much as possible, it's helpful to try to avoid having "guesses" about where they're going to land—or at least avoid sharing those guesses with your VIP. You want them to feel they can come to you to ask questions, get advice, and share updates about their journey as needed, without feeling like you're suggesting they pick a specific identity or looking for "evidence" to support a specific hypothesis. Remind them that they are in control here. While I know there may be moments of stress or frustration during this process, it's important to keep conversation open and make sure your VIP feels seen and supported by you along the way. This brings us to our next Joy Exercise!

JOY EXERCISE: WEATHER REPORTS

If your VIP is exploring many different identity, name, or pronoun options, come up with an easy and fun way for them to communicate where they're at with you. I've seen rotating signs with names on them, pronoun pins that include a directional arrow, or something like a morning "weather report" for them to share that there's a 50 percent chance of "he" today but an outlook of "they" over the weekend. Whatever it is, find a way to show them that you are not just tolerating but *enjoying* being along for the ride with them.

To close out this chapter, I'll remind you of the coming-out timelines we discussed in chapter 1. This journey isn't going to be simple or linear, and there isn't a prescribed timeline or a preset order of steps for how long things will take and what will be required to make your VIP feel comfortable. Rather, it's going to be a long and winding road moving forward, backward, sideways, and sometimes stopping altogether. Your VIP may have moments of stress, moments of doubt about their identity, or moments of questioning, and it's important that you focus on listening first. Give them a safe space to question and explore without feeling like your goal is figuring out if they're "really trans."

You and your VIP are on this journey together, but make sure they know they're in the driver's seat—and remember that unlike most actual road trips, you don't have to know exactly where you're going to start an adventure.

3

COMING OUT
AT HOME

Creating a Safe Home Environment
and Talking to Family Members

When your VIP first comes out, it may take some time for them to feel comfortable and ready to share their story with their broader community. Even if they aren't out to anyone except you and the people they live with, there are things you can do to help make your home environment as safe and supportive as possible. In fact, if they are only out to a small group of people, it is even *more* crucial that you have a home environment where they feel seen, because they aren't likely to be getting that anywhere else right now.

This chapter will walk you through a number of strategies for speaking to family members with different levels of understanding or support and explore how your whole family can fit in to building a supportive home environment both physically and psychologically.

Building a safe environment can involve simple things like making sure to use the right name and pronouns when you're in safe company or fun things like allowing your VIP to get home from school and change into clothes that feel more affirming. It might also look like changing some of the decorations in your home to remove their old name or old photographs.

BUILDING A SAFE PHYSICAL SPACE IN YOUR HOME

If your VIP is your child or lives with you, there are a few things you'll want to talk through together with the overall goal of figuring out how to make sure they feel seen as they are in your home. Here are a few potential questions to talk through with your VIP, as well as potential answers you might get.

How do you feel about seeing pictures of yourself from before you came out?

I know my own answer has evolved over time. I don't mind seeing pictures of myself as a little kid, especially given how cute I was and how different I looked then. Those pictures don't make me uncomfortable and I'm fine knowing that they are up in my parents' house, my grandma's house, and so on. However, I did not want to see pictures from my teenage years for a while. They felt more fresh, and when I looked at them I could see the pain in my eyes from the performance I was putting on every day, waiting to figure out who I was and share it with the people around me. Those pictures didn't reflect a part of me I was proud of or comfortable with, and I didn't appreciate seeing them around the house. Over time, I've gotten to a place where I don't have a specifically visceral reaction to them, but I also know that I have lots of new pictures with my family that are *way* better.

The answer to this question is very specific to the individual and may even change over time. Your VIP may say they find the pictures funny or that they don't carry any particular weight for them and they don't mind them staying up at all. Conversely, it may be a no across the board to any old pictures because they remind them of a more challenging, less authentic time or make them uncomfortable. Not sure what pictures to hang up instead? Get ready for our next Joy Exercise!

JOY EXERCISE: FAMILY PHOTOS

Though it may feel sad to take certain pictures down, this is also a delightful opportunity for a new source of joy for your family. Once your VIP has found a "look" they feel comfortable enough with, set aside some time to take new photos. Book a family photo shoot with an LGBTQ+ friendly photographer or become a tourist in your hometown and discover old and new favorite places to take pictures together where you all feel at your best.

Do you like the room you have? Are there any things you'd like to change about it?

When decorating a child's room and filling it with toys, clothes, and decorations, there are certain cultural norms about what rooms should look like for boys and for girls. Because the differences between boy colors/hobbies and girl colors/hobbies is entirely social, your VIP may not care about having their room be a "boy color" or having princess-themed bedsheets, and their coming out isn't a guarantee that what they need is a total bedroom redesign.

Some young people, especially those who are not out in other areas of their life, may find feelings of comfort or belonging in adding some more traditionally feminine or masculine touches to their space. Rather than leading questions like "Would you like us to make your room into a boy's room?" ask what changes would make them happy. Make sure to continually emphasize the focus of happiness. Your goal is not to make sure they do everything possible to feel "enough like a girl/boy to be accepted" but rather to make sure they know that there's not one way to be a girl/boy and that they deserve to be accepted exactly as they are.

Would you like to put things with your chosen name around the house?

This is a part of a larger conversation about how and when they're ready to come out, but it may be a small act of validation to have things around the house that include their chosen name if your home decor includes their old name or the names of your other children. Your VIP might not be comfortable with others potentially seeing and asking questions about the new name, so it's important to ask and make sure you're on the same page.

Curating a safe physical space is important piece of creating overall acceptance, but the physical space makes less of a difference if it isn't filled with supportive people. There are a variety of people who may be in your home, and another important piece is helping get them all on board, whatever their starting point may be.

HELPING YOUR VIP COME OUT TO OTHER PEOPLE

There are several ways you can help someone come out, largely depending on who your VIP is and what their relationship to you is. The most crucial thing is to *ask* what you can do to support them. Every person has different needs, and every relationship your VIP has is different too. You wouldn't help them come out to a teacher the same way you'd help them come out to their mother.

Another important note, which I have said before and will continue to drive home, is that you should never, ever disclose someone's identity without their explicit permission. Even if it feels like it would probably be helpful, it is always better to just ask first. Note that these tips aren't trans-specific; they're just ways to help someone prepare for an important and sometimes scary conversation. You can apply these skills anywhere.

Be a Sounding Board and Help Your VIP Practice Their "Speech"

Many coming-out conversations start a bit like speeches, and you can help the person write or practice the words they're going to say. Even just the words "I'm trans" can be so hard to say for the first time, so let them say it to you. Say it with them. Chant it. Dance around the room singing it. (Keeping in mind, of course, whatever level of professionalism your role with your VIP requires.) The point is to help them become comfortable with whatever they're planning to say. Another way to help is to prompt them with some practice questions they might need to answer and help them come up with good responses.

Be "On Call" for Your VIP, Even If You Know They Won't Need It

The level to which you will be "on call" for your VIP is once again based on your relationship with them, as well as how you anticipate the conversation going. It's important to leave room for people to surprise us, but it's equally important to be realistic in your planning. I would like to live in a world where I don't need to write even a single sentence about how to prepare for someone to get thrown out of their home, but that still happens at the time I'm writing this, so I should talk about it.

If you're genuinely worried about something like this happening, help them come up with a plan for what to do, where to go, whom to call, and so on. If it's appropriate and you feel comfortable doing so, you can offer them a couch to crash on if they need it. For some people, it's important to come up with these plans, so help them even if you know things aren't going to go that badly. When my good friend came out, I made sure he knew there was a bed for him at my house if he needed it, knowing full well he wouldn't. Having a safety net, even if you know they likely won't need it, makes that huge leap feel much less scary, so there's never any harm in having a plan. A much less extreme version of this plan is to just stay by your phone or make plans to go to lunch so you're ready to help them debrief and decompress, however the conversation went. Even if it went great, there's a lot of processing that needs to happen that you as a support system can help walk with them through (if they want/need to).

Be in the Room with Your VIP

Being present when someone comes out can help in several ways. Primarily, you can be there to answer questions that may come up so your VIP doesn't need to worry about having all the answers prepared right away. In situations where you're more concerned about how someone is going to react, your presence will serve as a preventative buffer; with another person present, someone who might otherwise have reacted negatively may take more time to think about their words. Though their opinion may not change, the way they deliver it will, which can help lessen the blow and prevent them from saying something that can't be taken back.

Offer to Speak to the Parties Afterward to Help Answer Their Questions

Being available to field questions afterward is another simple thing that removes some of the burden from the person who is coming out. Trans folks who come out are often immediately labeled the "designated educator." Everyone who feels confused by their transition, no matter how well (or not) they know the trans person, comes to ask every question and expects perfect answers and infinite patience. You certainly don't need to have every answer either, but what you can be is someone who has resources such as documentaries, articles, or books ready to share. (I know I can think of at least one great book to recommend!) Not only does this take away the stress of your VIP feeling like they need to go into coming out prepared to have answers to every question that might come up, but you've created a controlled environment where people can express their thoughts, feelings, and reactions to someone other your VIP. People need time to react, process, and learn without creating additional stress for the transgender person. We'll talk later about why taking private space to react is crucial for supporting your VIP, but in this context just remember that your VIP doesn't need a blow-by-blow report of every question asked or tear shed; they likely just need to know that the parties are learning as best they can.

Tell the Relevant Parties for Your VIP

Telling people on behalf of your VIP is helpful because it gives people a controlled environment to react, respond, and ask questions. Coming out is extremely emotionally exhausting, and sometimes trans people—certainly myself included—get to a point where we run out of steam and stop feeling willing or able to have the same conversation over and over again. The most important thing to continue to remember is that you should *never* do this without asking, and you shouldn't assume that being asked to do it for one person means you should do it for everyone. In other words, if your VIP asks you to talk to their grandparents for them, this doesn't necessarily mean they want you to tell the entire extended family without them. Again, you don't have to be an expert to have these conversations; you just need to have some resources ready or explain to people how to find reliable resources on their own.

Like all the other suggestions I give in this book, please remember that these are a handful of common strategies that can be really helpful for *some* people in *some* situations. You can use these as potential blueprints for support with your VIP, but it's important to find a strategy that feels right for both of you.

FAQ: WHAT DO I DO IF MY VIP DOESN'T WANT ME TO TELL A SPECIFIC PERSON?

To start off, it's okay to acknowledge that this may be confusing or frustrating to you, but you should be selective about how much of that frustration you share with your VIP. We'll talk about this more in depth in chapter 5, but the gist is that you want to avoid sending the message that it is frustrating to you when your VIP shares they aren't comfortable with a specific person, because if you express that frustration, they may hesitate to come to you with these concerns again.

If your VIP requests that you not tell someone, it's vitally important to respect your VIP's wishes as this will violate their trust in a way that may not be easy to restore. If there is a concern or a very good reason that requires you to tell that specific person, sit down with your VIP first to explain why they need to know.

If possible, it is best to address requests for privacy from an information-gathering perspective. There are many reasons why your VIP may not want to come out to a specific person:

- They may feel it would put them at risk for physical harm.
- They may feel the person would not be accepting.
- They may feel the person would not be understanding or might ask too many questions.
- They may feel the person would tell other people.
- They may not be sure how to tell them.
- They may be nervous to tell them but can't explain why.

There are many reasons your VIP may feel these things, many of which we explored in the section about the litmus test in chapter 2, but it can be something as big as religion and stated political beliefs or as small as what jokes someone laughs at or what TV shows they watch. Even if you personally don't have the impression that the person would be transphobic or unsupportive, it's important to find out what gave your VIP that impression so you can help them find a solution.

If telling the person is a legitimate safety concern, you may want to find a way to remove that person from contact with your VIP, as their identity cannot and will not always remain a secret, regardless of their intentions. This can be challenging to do, especially if this individual is very present in your life—a close friend, a family member, or even a spouse. It is not my place here to tell you what to do, but if your VIP feels they are at genuine risk for physical or psychological harm, you have an important opportunity to reassess how value aligned you are with this individual and decide how much that matters to you.

For concerns about privacy, if you believe the person won't be able to respect your VIP's privacy, it's best to wait until your VIP feels ready to share with others before telling this person. For all other concerns, it may be best for you to step in (with permission) and help your VIP come out to this person, and there are many ways for you to do so, as we discussed previously.

COMING OUT TO YOUNG CHILDREN

I often hear worries about how confusing trans and nonbinary identities may be for young children who have siblings, family members, or friends come out. To tell the truth, of every single person I came out to, my four-year-old cousin unquestionably had the easiest time understanding and switching to my new pronouns. Our conversation went something like this:

Me: Hi, Cousin!

Cousin: Hello!

Me: I wanted to let you know that my name is Ben now, and I'm a boy so you can call me he.

Cousin: Okay! Why?

Me: Well, being a girl didn't really fit anymore, and being Ben makes me happier.

Cousin: Cool! Do you want to play outside with me?

That cousin just turned nine and has a stuffed monkey who uses they/them pronouns. The reality is, it's quite easy for kids to understand nuances in gender identity. I saw this conversation play out with cousins and the kids I taught preschool to, and I have heard similar stories from other trans folks I know. A big part of the experience of being a kid is learning about all the rules that apply to the world: Look both ways before crossing the street; don't play with fire; go to sleep when it's dark; this is what it means to be a boy or a girl. The thing is, many of these rules are often broken for kids on special occasions. The experience of learning that sometimes a boy becomes a girl is about as shocking as the experience of getting to stay up late on New Year's Eve. Adults spend years learning these rules and seeing them reinforced by our communities, our media, and sometimes even our laws, so it's much harder for us to break the rules we've learned. For kids who haven't spent thirty years learning that someone cannot have a different gender identity, it's generally no big deal.

That said, kids are naturally curious beings, and there is a chance that you'll get some very interesting questions, so you and your VIP should plan out a handful of kid-friendly answers to questions about labels, bodies, or other things kids might ask, as well as explanations as to why certain questions aren't appropriate to ask.

One other important reminder is that kids may have a different view of privacy, and it's important to walk through with them that your VIP may not want them to talk about their identity or share their new name and pronouns with other people just yet. It's important to make sure the kids you're talking to know that even though they aren't allowed to talk about it yet, that doesn't mean your VIP's trans identity is something shameful or bad, they just aren't ready to talk to other people about it yet.

SPEAKING WITH UNSUPPORTIVE INDIVIDUALS

Far more challenging than telling young children are conversations with friends and family members who are not supportive. There are two main reasons someone may come across as unsupportive; they may seem similar but should be responded to in very different ways.

- They are struggling to understand why or how new name, label, or pronouns might be used, and they say unsupportive things with positive or neutral intentions.
- They are malicious toward the transgender community, do not make any effort to use the correct pronouns, or share questions/comments with hurtful intentions.

The second group is much louder and more prevalent on social media and other public discussions, so it's easy to assume they're a much larger group (hello, availability bias!), but the reality is that most folks we might categorize as unsupportive are firmly in the first category. Our focus with this group is going to be on creating judgment-free spaces where they can ask questions and practice new language.

Though for some of us, especially for younger people or for your VIP, these topics might be very comfortable and familiar, it's important to remember that for many people, this is a new concept that goes pretty firmly against what they've heard about how the world works for their whole lifetime. There is not reliable, easy access to accurate information, nor much effort to educate people, and media representation is a mixed bag of quality and accuracy. Many people are not set up for success in their learning about the trans community, and our goal is to welcome them in from wherever they're starting.

Take some time *without your VIP present* to ask these people what questions or concerns are on their mind and work through them as much as possible without judgment. Consider encouraging them to go *with you* to a support group like PFLAG. Your accompanying them may help them feel much more comfortable and may erase some guilt around learning "too late."

If they are generally supportive but struggle with getting your VIP's name and pronouns right, consider setting time aside (again, without your VIP present) to practice talking about your VIP with them and help correct each other on their name and pronouns.

Finding a balance between offering grace and patience and pushing for progress will be something you and your VIP can work out together, but once you find that balance, it is possible for anyone to change. I have family members who took years to stay on top of calling me "Ben" and "he," but with a significant amount of time and support from other family members, they were able to get there. (This might also be a great place to bring up the misgendering jar or spray bottle that we mentioned in the first chapter!)

DEALING WITH HATEFUL FAMILY MEMBERS

Many of us have likely had to deal with people in our families who are all manner of hateful. Maybe it's racist Uncle Dave who still gets invited to the family cookout because he makes the best burgers. Maybe it's Grandma, who makes homophobic "jokes" every chance she gets but gets a pass because "That's just Grandma."

Whoever they are, whatever they do or say, we have been told that family is family no matter what—blood is thicker than water, loyalty, all that jazz.

But what *is* family? You might define it in a number of ways: people you're related to by blood or marriage, people you have a shared history with, people you've known your whole life, people you love and who love you.

That last one is the most important. *Love* is what makes a family, and if someone is bringing hate or malice to your Thanksgiving table and not facing any consequences, that person is not family. When people don't face social repercussions for their actions, it gives them permission to continue with what they're saying or doing. As much as we'd like to think that just trying to avoid politics at holiday gatherings is a neutral act involving the same sacrifice for everyone, that's usually not true: To your VIP, refusing to confront someone who is actively malicious toward them means that you are picking that person's side.

At the end of the day, someone is going to be uncomfortable or unhappy. It's either going to be your VIP, who is uncomfortable or unhappy because they feel unseen and disrespected just for trying to be themselves, or it's going to be your family member, who found out that if they keep saying slurs or intentionally misgendering your VIP for the purpose of being malicious, they're no longer going to be welcome.

Though some people in your family may tell you to avoid rocking the boat or to not "make it political," politics aren't what they used to be. This isn't a debate over the school budget or road maintenance; this is about whether someone should be allowed to exist. My life as a transgender person has been made completely political (against my will, I should add), and that means that while supporting transgender people is considered a political act, at the end of the day it is simply about letting someone live their life.

I want to say this as loud and clear as possible: It is okay to uninvite someone from a holiday. It is okay to stop attending gatherings that include that person. It is okay to let that person know that they aren't welcome to be in your VIP's life until they learn how to do so with kindness and respect.

Some family members may ask why you're "choosing to do this" based on the notion that the malicious family member is obviously not going to change, so why can't you just accept it and deal with it? Let me be clear: *Everyone* has the ability to change and grow if they want to. When asked why you are choosing not to accept how this family member is, ask instead why this family member is choosing not to stop being hateful toward someone they are supposed to love. Emphasize that you are willing to welcome this person back in if they are willing to treat your VIP with basic kindness and respect. Other members of your family should put pressure on the malicious person to stop being malicious, not on your VIP to stop being upset about the malice.

CHOSEN FAMILY

There may be people in your family who do not support you in this, and they will have to make a similar choice between you and your VIP and the hateful or unkind member of your family. It's an extremely hard reality that LGBTQ+ people are used to being cut off from our families, whether it's because they cast us out right away or because we decided that we weren't receiving love and respect from them and found our own distance. If there is a malicious person in your family who makes family gatherings challenging or even unsafe for your VIP, your VIP is likely trying to find ways to create significant distance between themselves and that person as soon as they're able, and your willingness or unwillingness to help stand up to that person may determine what side of that distance you're on.

Distancing yourself from your family of origin can be exceptionally challenging and painful, and I want to highlight the notion of a "chosen family," which is a really beautiful concept often occurring within the queer community that emphasizes the fact that families are built on love, not always on blood, and that our families can include partners, roommates, neighbors, friends, and other people who greet us and see us with love. As you gain additional distance from members of your family who do not treat you and your VIP with love, try to focus on the new, loving relationships and family you can find and build around yourself.

While you may not be able to find perfect solutions to dealing with old family photos or challenging family members, showing your VIP that you are on their side and ready to go to bat for them is crucial. The love and support you surround them with acts as armor against the challenges the world may throw at them, and as much as possible it's crucial for your VIP to have a safe space where those challenges can't reach them, at least for a little while.

4

COMING OUT IN
YOUR COMMUNITY

At this point, I think we're feeling pretty good within the walls of our homes and in spaces that are relatively controlled, like family gatherings with trusted individuals or support group meetings. At some point, your VIP will feel ready to embark on a journey as their authentic self into the great wide world. This might happen shortly after they come out to you, or it might happen weeks, months, or even years later. There are a lot of feelings that may come up related to that decision, and we'll explore them more in depth in chapter 6, but it's key to understand that everyone has a timeline that feels right for them, and you should not try to force anyone to come out publicly if they don't feel ready.

As with any other unpredictable situation, one of the best things you can do to be as ready as possible is to create a coming-out plan!

CREATING YOUR COMING-OUT PLAN

Once your VIP shares that they are ready to begin coming out to a broader group of people, it's important to make sure that you're on the same page about what they are and aren't comfortable with—and to do so *before* you get thrown into those situations. In the following sections are lists of questions to discuss with your VIP. Remember, this is not a one-time conversation—you'll want to revisit these questions your VIP's comfort zone evolves.

Questions about Coming Out to Extended Family

- Who would your VIP like to tell themselves?
- Who would your VIP like you to tell for them?
- How would you like to share with more distant family members?

Questions about Coming Out to the Broader Community

- Is your VIP comfortable with you sharing about their identity? If so, in what situations (i.e., when relevant to support another, only if they'll be meeting, always, etc.)?
- Is your VIP comfortable with being introduced as a support or resource to other trans youth and their families?
- Is your VIP okay with *new* connections learning about their identity, or would they prefer to share only with people who knew them before they came out?

Questions about Answering Questions

- What kind of questions is your VIP comfortable answering?
- What kind of questions is your VIP comfortable with you answering for them?
- What kind of questions would your VIP prefer be avoided altogether?
- Are there any examples of media or public figures who your VIP feels reflect their identity to help others develop a deeper understanding of their experiences?

As you may be expecting, it can quickly become a bit of a hassle to share the news with your broader community—trying to make a list of all the people who know your VIP can quickly become a seemingly endless task. One-on-one coming-out conversations take a significant amount of time and effort and you are only one person, but there are other ways to spread the news. Below is a sample letter to your community that can be sent as snail mail, email, or a social media post to help share the news and provide resources to those who need them. It's important to make sure this letter feels authentic to your VIP, though they don't need to be the one to send it.

Sample Letter

Hello friends and family!

We're writing to you with some exciting updates on our VIP. VIP has shared with us that they identify as [VIP's identity] and will now be using the name [VIP's name] and the pronouns [VIP's pronouns]. If this is an identity you're unfamiliar with, here are some helpful resources to learn more:

- *Resources should be specific to your VIP's identity, so include here some resources that can help people learn more about your VIP's identity. Check the resources with your VIP to make sure they paint a complete, accurate picture of the information they'd like your community to receive.*

If your VIP would like to, they can share their personal experience with their identity and discovery journey to help your community better understand, but it's important to emphasize that this is not by any means required of them.

Going forward, we will show love and respect to our VIP by doing our best to make their new name and pronouns a part of our vocabulary. We understand that this may take time and practice and appreciate your effort to make sure our VIP feels seen and supported. If you would like an opportunity to practice VIP's new name and pronouns, feel free to give us a call and we can practice together.

If your VIP has any specific requests about things like nicknames, old stories, pictures, or questions they are/aren't comfortable answering you can share them here as well.

We are so proud of our VIP for learning something new about themselves and sharing it with the world, and though it may take time to fully understand their experience, we are able to meet them with love and respect unwaveringly, and we hope you will be too. We're sharing this with you because you are a member of our VIP's community, and we want to have as broad a support system as possible for our VIP as they continue their journey. If you have any other questions, please reach out to *whoever would you like to direct questions to.*

P.S. If you're looking for more resources, we've got a perfect book to lend you!

Now that your letter has been sent or your calls have been made, your VIP might be feeling a bit adrift—wondering what reactions people are having to this news and whether their community will support them. This is an excellent opportunity for a coming-out party—and no, I'm not talking about an 1800s-style debutante ball, although there are quite a few parallels—I'm talking about our next Joy Exercise!

JOY EXERCISE: COMING-OUT CELEBRATION

Though at times stressful, coming out publicly can and should be a very exciting time. There are lots of ways you can celebrate this, and it's important to make sure your VIP knows that you love and support them as they are and as they continue to grow into themselves along this journey. One of my favorite types of celebrations I've seen during the coming-out process is a gender re-reveal party that includes traditional gender reveal party decorations and activities, but with the correct identity of your VIP. I've also seen truly adorable trans versions of a baby shower in which there are some silly games and activities followed by sharing of gifts that a person may need as they enter this new part of their life (like a first makeup or shaving kit).

There are many ways this celebration could look, and it should be planned according to what feels right to your VIP. If they're an extrovert looking forward to the positive attention, a big celebration may be perfect. If they don't love big parties or don't want to announce their transition yet, it's likely best to do something smaller. It could even be something as simple as buying them one of those "It's a girl!" Hallmark cards or replacing some kind of decoration that displays their name with a new version with their new name. If you'd like some other ideas for small celebrations fit for a more introverted VIP, check out the Joy Exercise in chapter 1.

There isn't one specific right way to celebrate; what matters is that you find some authentic way to mark the occasion and continue to emphasize to your VIP that you're on their team.

LEGAL NAME AND GENDER MARKER CHANGES

At some point, your VIP may want to go through the process of legally changing their name and gender marker. By the time I finished the process and got my last legal document back in the mail, I was seriously considering joining Cirque du Soleil because of how good I'd gotten at jumping through hoops. Though state and local policies vary, there are a few things most states have in common about name and marker change laws.

In general, your first step in legally changing your name is typically a bit of paperwork and your end result is a notarized court-ordered name change document you can bring with you to the DMV, social security office, and passport office. To get from point A to point B, there are a few different steps, depending on what state you live in. Some states—like Connecticut, where I'm from—require you to make an appointment and visit your local appellate court to explain the name change. Other states require that you publish an announcement of the name change in your local newspaper.

Once all is said and done and you've got your document, you'll be given the option to receive multiple notarized copies of your name change order. I would recommend having three or four copies, because some agencies may hang onto that paperwork for a longer time while they process it. You should be able to request more if you need them later on.

Changing legal gender markers tends to require more hoops, and again, exactly what these are will depend on where you live. In some places, you need a letter from at least one medical professional to prove you are taking steps to make your transition permanent. There is also variation from state to state about which markers you're allowed to use. In some states it's just M or F, but many states are beginning to adopt an additional marker, X, for nonbinary people.

I would recommend changing information on official documents like a driver's license or passport after your VIP's name and marker are changed—if both are things they're interested in, which they may not be. Given how time consuming and expensive the process to change those documents can be, it's best to try to make all the changes at once.

It is also worth noting that there are many resources to support trans people with the costs or navigating the hoops of these processes. Microgrants are often available to cover expenses, and organizations like the Transgender

Legal Defense and Education Fund can help you find legal representation if you need it. It is worth researching what specific resources exist in your area to help you with any barriers you may experience. If you're eager to find resources, jump to chapter 7 for an in-depth guide to finding community, state, and national level resources.

NAVIGATING PUBLIC RESTROOMS

One of the most common fears I hear from trans people and their families involve public bathrooms, and unfortunately these fears are sometimes warranted. The fear of someone deciding that we don't belong in there and either maliciously or "helpfully" pointing out the other bathroom's location (or something worse) is a nightmare that many trans people have at some point in their lives seen come true. I tell you this not to scare you, but to help you understand why your VIP may be stressed about this and what you can do to support them.

No matter where I am, when I go to the bathroom, I watch to see if anyone is watching me go in, and I take stock of how many other people are in the bathroom to determine whether it's safe for me. If I feel there's a chance someone might take issue with me being there, I'll grab a paper towel, blow my nose, and walk out. When I traveled to visit family in North Carolina—at the time the home of the most infamous of the "bathroom bills"—I used to do anything it took to avoid needing to go to the bathroom in public. That usually entailed not drinking any water on days I knew we were planning to leave the house, which more than once resulted in me nearly fainting from dehydration.

While there are many detractors who state that allowing trans people to use appropriate restrooms is a danger to society, the harmful claims these people make tend to be based on fear and transphobia (both implicit and explicit) rather than facts. A groundbreaking study at the Williams Institute at UCLA looked at communities that had trans-positive bathroom bills, allowing people to use any bathroom they wanted, and communities that did not. The researchers then traced the police records to see if there was any increase in incidents of bathroom-related crime and found no correlation between the number of crimes and laws allowing trans people to use their correct restrooms. In short, when trans people are allowed to use the bathroom, nothing bad happens!

As time has gone on, I've found ways to feel safer and more comfortable in bathrooms. The thing that helped the most at first was talking to my dad about it. When he found out I had been going days without water because of how scared I was, we came up with a signal that I could send to him if I was going to the bathroom and felt nervous or unsafe. He'd come with me and just wash his hands and make sure I knew nothing was going to happen to me. As I've gotten more confident in my ability to pass, I send that signal less and less often, though there are still times where I make a judgment call when I don't feel quite comfortable. This is an important highlight—my comfort and safety in the bathroom was not confidence based; I had and continue to have legitimate concerns about my safety and need to act accordingly.

If your VIP identifies as nonbinary or an identity other than male or female, there are additional concerns in choosing a bathroom given that neither one feels quite right. For both nonbinary youth and binary trans youth who just don't feel quite comfortable in public bathrooms, there are a few steps you can take to alleviate those stressors. For an immediate solution, start developing a list of businesses around you that have single-use or gender-neutral bathrooms, as these bathrooms alleviate most or all safety concerns. Starbucks, for example, is known among trans folks as a safe haven because all their locations have gender-neutral bathrooms. In some places, single-use bathrooms still have gendered signs on the door, which is very silly to me! For a longer-term solution, consider reaching out to those businesses to suggest they make their single-use bathrooms gender neutral to be more welcoming to the trans and nonbinary community.

Developing systems like this has helped me become more comfortable in both restrooms and public spaces in general. When I'm not in my own city with familiar safe havens, I often use tools like the Open to All feature on Yelp, which allows businesses to indicate on their online review profiles if they are specifically welcoming to LGBTQ+ patrons. This isn't to say that businesses that don't have that flag are homophobic or transphobic, but it makes me feel much more comfortable when I can take the guesswork out of picking somewhere for lunch in an unfamiliar city. There are also smartphone apps such as Refuge Restroom to locate gender-neutral bathrooms nearby.

FACING CHALLENGES

As much as I wish we could shield your VIP from any and all rude or hateful speech, the reality is that (at least at the time when I am writing this book) the current political climate is an extremely polarized and present one that no one is able to be truly insulated from. It may help you to think through in advance what you might do or say if someone says something to or about your VIP in public. If you want to be an active ally both to your own VIP and to trans folks in general, I would suggest putting to use any active bystander training you may have had, whether in high school or two weeks ago in your required HR training. If there is a situation where it appears someone is harassing a person because of their gender or sexuality, find a way to intervene. Spill water on the offending party, find an authority to come and help, or step in directly if there are no safety concerns. People on the internet love to share "hilarious" videos of trans people trying to stand up for themselves when people use the wrong pronouns or block them from entering a restroom, with bystanders are watching, laughing, or filming, but not helping. In many of these videos, it is clear the person being harassed is getting extremely upset. I can only imagine how differently those videos would have gone if someone had put down their phone and helped them stand up for themselves.

While there is no possible way I can tell you absolutely everything that can and will happen as your VIP enters the world as their authentic self, I hope we've created a strong toolkit that you can use to support your VIP as much as possible. As I'll continue to drive home, the strongest item in your toolkit is your ability to check in with and listen to your VIP. Their comfort levels may change from day to day, from person to person, or from place to place, and one size certainly does not fit all in figuring out how to be an impactful ally. Coming out is a lifelong process—there will always be new people who do not yet know your VIP's story or identity—and your VIP will undoubtedly have changing preferences and comfort zones as they mature, so buckle up, let them know that you've got their back, and enjoy the ride.

II

BUILDING STRONG FOUNDATIONS

5

PROCESSING YOUR FEELINGS

At the end of the last chapter, I told you to enjoy the ride, and I think the metaphor of a roller coaster actually works quite nicely here. As with any roller coaster, there are going to be quite a few emotions that come up along this journey: Anticipation before big conversations, twists and turns where you feel like you're just barely hanging on to the cart, and, of course, the depth-defying stomach-churning drop. Perhaps you've already had that drop moment. Perhaps you're in the middle of it right now. Perhaps you feel it's still coming. That moment is terrifying, no two ways about it, but let's continue with our analogy for just a moment longer: The reason we feel safe getting on a roller coaster is that even if it's our first time, we know that roller coaster track was designed by a group of experienced professionals with everyone's safety in mind. Thousands of families just like ours have ridden this loop before and made it out the other side with smiles on their faces.

It's reasonable to have lots of feelings, and we'll talk through strategies for processing many of those feelings, but I want to make sure you know that you are not the first person to be feeling these things, and you won't be the last either.

GROUNDING IN RING THEORY

Before we jump into the more specific fears and feelings that individuals often have when their VIPs come out, I want to talk about those feelings on a more general level with one of my favorite frameworks: ring theory.

Ring theory was designed by Susan Silk and Barry Goldman to talk about showing support for individuals at the center of a tragedy, but it lends itself very nicely to this conversation as well.[1] Essentially, when something happens to someone—in our case, when they come out—they are at the center of a series of concentric rings. The outer rings are made up of the people they know, with the closer rings representing those who are closest to them. Parents might be in the first closest ring, then other family members, friends, and teachers or other people involved in their life.

When you talk to someone in a ring that is closer to the center than you, it's most appropriate to direct comfort. When you're hoping to vent your feelings or seek support, it's best to reach out to someone further from the center than you are. Using the common example of someone with cancer—though to be clear, transgender identities are in *no way* related to/similar to having cancer—if your VIP was diagnosed with cancer, would you come to them to tell them how hard it is for you that they have cancer? You're probably thinking that that would be quite inappropriate, and you'd be right! They are more affected by the situation than you are, and hearing about how hard it is for you is only going to make it harder on them.

We can apply the same logic to talking about your VIP's journey—but I also want to add an extremely important caveat: This is in terms of *communicating* your feelings, not *having* feelings. No one, least of all me, can tell you what you should and shouldn't feel. We can't control our feelings, but we can control how we respond to and share those feelings.

In general, if you say something that causes another person to be upset, what's your natural emotional response going to be? Guilt! From an adult's perspective, I'm able to understand that sometimes people are upset by things that need to be said and that I'm not always responsible for other people's feelings, but these insights have been gained over years of emotional development and maturity. Young people don't have those years of experience under their belt and are much more likely to jump to feeling guilty if they shared their identity with you and then they see or hear that it's causing you stress or pain.

Two things can also be true at once: that you love and support your child and that you might be having a challenging emotional reaction to them coming out. Especially if they are very young, your VIP may not be able to hold both of those truths at the same time and may worry that your reaction means you aren't supportive of them.

The younger they are, the truer this is. If your VIP is in their twenties or older, there is likely opportunity for *some* productive conversation, but I want to encourage you to be selective about what and when you choose to share with them. Even as a trans adult, with the amount of hate being thrown my way from every corner of the country, I need every unconditional ally in my corner that I can get.

For all these reasons, it's important to find sources other than your VIP to process your reactions with. Again, this is not to say that you cannot have these feelings, just that your VIP is probably not the best audience for them.

For the rest of this chapter, we're going to walk through several of the most common feelings and concerns I've heard in my decade of talking with parents about these topics, and I'll discuss common questions for reflection, research studies, or additional thoughts that might bring some comfort. I encourage you to really take time to sit with these feelings and these questions, as there is often much more under the surface of our reactions and fears than we expect. Consider talking through your thoughts with a partner, friend, or therapist, or taking time to write out your responses in a journal.

As we're looking through our variety of thoughts and feelings, I also want us to be intentional about noticing the differences between identifying *emotions* and identifying *excuses*. We want to make sure we're giving space to our feelings but that we aren't justifying holding back support for our VIPs. For example, an emotion might be feeling sad that you can no longer use the familiar nickname your VIP has been using for years; an excuse might be that you can't call them their new name consistently because you're just so used to their old name or nickname. By working through the emotion, we can break down the excuse, but make sure you identify the difference as you walk through what you are feeling.

COMMON FEARS AND CONCERNS

Fear for Your VIP's Safety

People who love their VIPs and have heard how dangerous or challenging it can be to be a member of the trans community often have fears for their safety or future. We'll talk more later about how to talk to your VIP about this and explore strategies they can use to keep themselves safe, but here I want to address this worry.

Unlike other fears or worries I'm going to address in this chapter, I can't disprove this one. It is extremely reasonable to worry about how the world is going to treat your VIP and want to protect them from that. Depending on how old your VIP is, they likely have had many of the same thoughts and decided already it was worth the risk to be able to live authentically. I decided early on that while I would be safer as a cisgender woman than as a transgender man, an inauthentic life was not one worth living. Even now, as I am writing this, when anti-trans sentiment, legislation, and violence is at an all-time high, I still feel firmly that the risks are worth it to get to live as I am. If your VIP is younger, they are still finding and living their truth, and we don't want the world to be a reason they can't do that.

Though it certainly can feel like it would be easier to change is your VIP's trans identity, that isn't possible and will only make your VIP feel unsupported. So it's best to direct your energy at trying to change the world to make it a safe place for your VIP to be themselves. While this feels daunting, it is absolutely possible, and incredible progress has been made in the past few decades—in huge part due to passionate allies like yourself! The fact that this book was published by a traditional publishing company, that you (probably) bought this book at a major book retailer, that you can read it on the train or talk about it with a friend is a result of increases in visibility, education, and support from allies and activists around the world. We will talk more later in the book about how to go about changing the world, but for now I want to make sure you have a more productive way to frame and respond to those thoughts as they come up.

The best way to deal with this concern is to consider this question: Of the things you're afraid of your VIP experiencing in the world, what can you contribute to changing?

If your fears for their safety are based on dangerous or unsupportive laws in the state they live in, you have a few different paths. Within unsupportive states, there are often metropolitan areas finding major and minor ways to resist these laws and build supportive environments, and it may be worth looking at what local community resources are available. You can also look to national groups like Elevated Access, a volunteer group of pilots helping fly families and individuals to states where they are able to continue accessing their care. While it may be more challenging, if your VIP lives with you and you are considering relocating, know that you are not alone—it's estimated that between 130,000 and 260,000 trans individuals had already fled their home states as of June 2023.[2] Because of how quickly and dramatically this landscape changes, we aren't going to spend much time discussing how and where to move, but resources like Erin Reed's Legislative Risk Map can help provide updated information on the safest states to live in and travel to.

Earlier in the book, I mentioned availability bias, which means we believe things happen more or less often than they do based on how often we see or hear about it. We don't often see representations in media or people in real life who are just regular trans adults living their lives, but there are millions (yes, millions plural) of us out there: trans people with spouses, with careers, with children, with homes, with dreams, with futures. There is so much trans joy and success in the world, it's just not something we see every day. While trans trauma seems to dominate the news and entertainment, that does not mean it's the only possibility for trans lives. I would encourage you to find a local LGBTQ+ center in your area and visit with your VIP to meet trans adults who can be *positive possibility models*. The more similar they are to your VIP, the better. Finding someone with a similar career path or of the same race or religion can be extremely helpful in allowing you and your VIP to see how it is possible for them to grow up and become a thriving trans adult.

Grief about "Losing" a Child

Grief is an emotion I hear exceptionally often from parents in particular, often described as a "mourning period" or as "losing a daughter/son but gaining a son/daughter." There's a lot to unpack here, but I'd like to start with some questions to reflect on:

1. What are you losing?
2. Did you truly have those things before your VIP came out? How do you know they're really gone?
3. Do young people always meet our expectations or follow the paths we imagine for them?
4. What are your favorite things about your VIP? How many of those are related to specific gender roles?
5. How much of your own familial relationships were based on your gender identity? Were there traditions you didn't particularly enjoy or ones you wished you were a part of?

These questions are extremely specific to you and your VIP, and your answers are likely to be deeply personal, so rather than telling you what I might think the "right answer" is, I'll share some additional guidance for reflecting on these questions. I know it may feel big and scary to try to make a list of everything that you feel you're losing now that your VIP has come out, but this can (for some people) be a helpful tool. Maybe it's things you like to do together, or things you're able to talk about, hobbies or interests you share, or dreams you have for their future like walking them down the aisle. Once you have this list, going through each item more in depth may help you find some peace.

For each thing on that list that you feel you're losing, I want you to think about how you *knew* you had it before. Is it because your VIP told you so or something you do together every week? Maybe it's something you expected to have because "everyone does it" or it feels obvious. How do you know for sure that these things are gone? Has your VIP told you they don't want to do something anymore, or are you just expecting them to be completely different now?

While we're on the topic of thinking of all the parts of your VIP, I want to bring in some positive reminders. Think about all your favorite things about your VIP: their personality traits, habits, things you share, or anything else. I know right now your VIP's entire identity might feel wrapped up in their gender, but it's important to remember that they are a whole person with a rich inner and outer life and a personality that is not exclusively gender based.

If you're still struggling with the fear that your entire relationship is going to change, I want you to go even further inward and think about why this is so stressful for you. Think about your own childhood and your own familial relationships, which shape many of our emotional reactions and views of the world today. For many people in older generations, gender roles were an overwhelming factor in determining family relationships and roles, and it makes sense that you might assume this dynamic would carry over into your relationship with your VIP. But the reality is, it doesn't have to be that way. Relationships and cultures have evolved in so many ways to fit the expansion of gender roles and identities—and many cultures around the world originally *did* explore different gender roles and identities. This may feel like a new muscle, but being able to move into new ways of thinking about relationship dynamics is key to maintaining a trusting and authentic relationship with your VIP.

This brings up one of the most important overarching themes here: I have spoken with many, many trans people over the course of writing this book, and throughout my ten years of living in the world as a trans person, and many people talk at length about their relationships with their families. There are a variety of things that might change the relationship between a trans person and their family, but nothing impacts those changes as much as family support. Being supportive and respectful, and letting your VIP know you see them and you love them, will be what maintains and even strengthens your relationship.

The key takeaway from this exercise is that the young people we know and love, both transgender and cisgender, are going to spend their lives agreeing with us, disagreeing with us, disappointing us, making us proud, and surprising us. We can have as many preconceived notions as we want about what a person's life will look like and who they'll be, but, as I'm told they say in sports, "That's why they make you play the game." There's no 100 percent guarantee how anyone is going to turn out. Many, but certainly not all, of the expectations we have—careers, future partners, hobbies, and personalities—are based in gender identity, and even cisgender children may not fit those expectations. When someone comes out as trans or nonbinary, it's true that they may be rejecting many of those expectations all at once, and that can be a lot, but it's important to remember that young people (and adults too!) frequently defy our expectations and this is not specific to their trans identity.

I often hear about grief from trans youth who have heard their parents express these feelings and even trans adults who heard it from their parents years ago and have never been able to fully let it go. I want to strongly encourage you not to share these feelings with your VIP, and if you step into their shoes for a minute, the reason for this should be clear. Imagine you've spent part of or even your entire life feeling like something wasn't quite right, like the real you wasn't all the way there. You realize you're trans, you realize what you need to do to feel authentic, and you bide your time waiting until it feels safe and right to introduce the people around you to your true self. You finally come out and can live as yourself for the first time—dress how you want, be called what you want, live how you want. It's incredible. And amid that new joy, that brand-new realness, one of the people you love most tells you that it feels like you killed someone, that they don't know who you are and they miss the person who never really felt like you. To a young person already coming out into a world that is trying to crush them because of who they are, this is a devastating thing to hear. I'm not telling you that you can't *feel* this feeling—though I hope exploring the questions in this section helped with that—but I am *strongly* recommending that you do not talk to your VIP about this feeling. What they need from you now is to know that there is someone who sees them as they want to be seen and loves them as they *are*, not as they *were*.

I know it can be easy to feel acutely aware of all that you might be losing, but you are gaining a significant amount as well. Spend some time shifting your thoughts away from what's gone and try to brainstorm (both by yourself and with your VIP) all the things you're gaining and what you're excited to do together, as well as what traditions will continue.

Feeling Conflicted about Religion

Religion is a topic that can be very sticky. For some people, faith is a weapon used to demonize others and withhold love and support. For others, faith is a shield against a hateful world. The next myth I want to bust is that being religious and being LGBTQ+ are mutually exclusive.

While it's true that some people use religion as an excuse to oppress members of the LGBTQ+ community, others use it as justification for providing unequivocal love and support, and many LGBTQ+ people themselves are religious. I know that as a Jewish man, I can't go into other houses of worship to tell people what their faith means, and (hopefully) this book is being picked up by people coming from a wide variety of faith traditions. As such, I want to direct you toward Strong Family Alliance, which has created a specific resource page full of leading faith-based organizations to help you hear from people and leaders in your own specific religious community about what it means to them to be members of and allies to the LGBTQ+ community.[3]

Here are a few questions to reflect on as you navigate your concerns about religion:

1. What is the focus of your religion? Does it emphasize love and care for community members?
2. If specific lines of religious texts are challenging to you, do you take every line of that text literally or apply to present-day concerns, or only select lines?
3. If a religion that claims to be loving does not allow you to love your child, is it truly loving?

I can't go on your religious journey for you, and there are entire books devoted to these topics written by queer people and scholars from all manner of faith traditions, but I would like to share a little bit of my religious journey. Getting unequivocal support from my rabbi after coming out was crucial to establishing that my God loved me no matter what. Since then, seeing the numerous ways people chose to use Judaism as a force for change and social good has deeply reaffirmed for me that my faith sees and loves me as I am. A few years ago, I read a quote that stays with me to this day: "God blessed me by making me trans for the same reason God made wheat but not bread and fruit but not wine, so that humanity might share in the act of creation."[4] I do not feel like a mistake was made in my creation; I feel like I was created exactly as I was meant to be.

Feeling Conflicted about Science

One of the questions I often hear, especially when it comes to nonbinary and gender-expansive identities, is, how is it possible that biological sex is so simple and gender identity is so widely varied? While it's exceptionally convenient to think of biological sex as a pure binary—made up of people who are either exactly male or exactly female—that is far from the case scientifically. Here are a couple questions to reflect on:

1. What biological differences can you think of between those assigned female at birth and those assigned male at birth?
2. Thinking of every person you have ever met in those categories, do those differences show up in the exact same way every single time?

I hope you're realizing that while there are things that are true generally, they may not be exactly true every single time. Rather than a binary, biological sex is actually bimodal, which means there are things that are true on average but show up as a spectrum. Consider something like height: On average, it's true that those assigned male at birth are taller than those assigned female at birth, but I've seen the WNBA before—I know that isn't true for every single person.

Biological sex existing on a spectrum also means that there are people who fall in between the two averages, that there are many people with disorders of sex development (sometimes called being intersex), and that there are those who have sex characteristics outside of the traditional definitions of male and female, which might involve differences in reproductive capabilities, genitalia, or chromosomes.

So the scientific reality is that biological sex, just like gender identity, is far more nuanced than we may have been taught. There is also a growing body of literature supporting the existence of gender identity in the brain and affirming the identities of transgender people, but I'm not going to specifically focus on those studies here. While I could most likely collect enough studies to prove beyond a reasonable doubt that your VIP is telling the truth about their identity, I want to point back to one of my guiding principles: Your VIP is the leading expert on themselves, and no one knows them better than they do.

Fear That This Is Your Fault

If you're concerned with issues of blame or fault, it's important to start by considering this question: Do you view your VIP being transgender as a bad thing? While you might not actively think of it this way, emotions like blame, fault, or guilt only arise when we feel we've done something *wrong*, and I encourage you to spend some time sitting with this question.

I'm also going to share an emphatic no—trans and queer identities are neither causable nor preventable. There is nothing you did to bring this about, and there is nothing you could have done differently to stop this from happening.

Though there is not a large body of research around specifically when trans or queer identities develop, the research that does exist suggests that for many people it is ingrained from birth or before. There are also many studies about conversion efforts: attempts to change someone's identity to cisgender and/or heterosexual through a variety of (usually barbaric and often traumatizing) measures. Studies find across the board that these efforts are never effective in actually changing someone's experience of their identity; their only impact is to deepen internalized stigma and force people into marriages they wouldn't otherwise choose, as well as into depression, substance abuse, and worse.[5] To quote another of the great philosophers of our time, Lady Gaga: "Baby, I was born this way!"

From a scientific perspective, I should note that it is unlikely that there will be significant research into what causes a person to be trans or queer, and this is intentional. If we were able to exactly identify what it is that makes a person LGBTQ+, whether it's womb temperature, hormone exposure, or something else in their pre- or post-birth environment, how long do you think it would be before malicious individuals started developing "cures" or "preventions"? There is too much risk here for it to be worth investigating, and there are much bigger problems worth dedicating research time and dollars to.

All this is to say that it shouldn't matter—the only thing that's "your fault" here is that your VIP felt safe enough to share their identity with you, and that's nothing short of amazing.

Fear That Your VIP Might Regret It and That You're Making a Mistake in Supporting Them

Many politicians and conservative media figures have latched on to the concept of detransition, but it is something that happens exceedingly rarely.

The people you may have heard about who have detransitioned are likely members of a select group of individuals called "political detransitioners," who are often given large donations, book deals, and social media platforms and encouraged by right-wing organizations to travel around the country and speak out against the transgender community. We'll discuss more about medical-specific regret statistics in chapter 8, but for now I want to talk about detransition overall.

Let's say you aren't sure if your VIP is going to regret transitioning and you decide to hold back full support until they're older, wanting make sure they have time to decide if this is really who they are. I can tell you that although it does happen, from a statistical perspective, detransition is *extremely* rare. What is more likely to happen when you hold back support, regardless of how loving you are with your words and intentions, is that you'll send your VIP the message that you don't support them at all. Instead of feeling safe and empowered to think about and explore their identity, they're going to feel unsupported and isolated, with the fear that any thought or question they voice to you will be used as further evidence against supporting them. They aren't deciding if they're trans; they're deciding if you are worth having in their lives. I know this might sound harsh, but it is a reality I have seen play out time and time again with the trans folks I know who came out at a younger age and didn't get the support they needed.

The question reflect on here is: What is the worst-case scenario? What do you want to avoid?

Usually, when I ask people this question, they respond by telling me they are afraid their VIP may go through permanent changes they later regret and that they might feel uncomfortable in their body.

I agree that we'd generally like to avoid anything that causes someone to feel uncomfortable in their body, and I usually follow up this question by asking parents what the difference is between the type of discomfort they're worried their child *might* have in the future and the type of discomfort their child is currently experiencing. Although they may not have the words for it, these parents are afraid that their children will experience gender dysphoria later in life, and while this is possible, it is statistically *much* more likely that their current dysphoria will persist and worsen if it goes unaddressed.

I can't promise you that your VIP is 100 percent correct that what their identity is now is what it will be in thirty years, but what I can do is promise that whatever their identity is in thirty years, they're making note of how you show up for them *today*. If they do detransition (which, again, is unlikely), they will want your support in that, but if you have not established yourself as a supportive person to talk to about their gender identity, they're unlikely to feel comfortable talking to you about it. A notable lack of support has the ability to permanently damage love and trust in a relationship, and in my mind that's fairly close to a real worst-case scenario.

Fear That This Is a Trend

There are a variety of reasons why folks come to me with concerns that this might be a fad or a trend. Generally, it's either because they didn't see any "signs" before or because they know their VIP recently had someone else close to them (often a school friend) come out. If you're concern centers around the first one, recall our discussion in the section of chapter 2 that discusses what to do if you suspect your VIP is trans: In essence, there aren't always any signs. There is no one way someone can *look* trans; for myself, I wasn't the most masculine kid, nor did I tell my parents as a young child that I wanted to be a boy. There were no signs, and yet here I am ten years later, happy in my identity. In addition, some trans folks over-index on assigned gender roles before they come out to themselves or others as a way to prevent suspicions about our identities from developing before we're ready. In the months before I came out, I wore more dresses to school than at any other time in my life.

For the second one, there are a variety of explanations for the phenomenon you may have seen or heard about in which a whole friend group seems to come out as trans or LGBTQ+ around the same time. At school age, there are lots of reasons why someone might experience ostracism or bullying, many of which can be described as being noticeably different in some way. For reasons related and unrelated to our LGBTQ+ identities, queer people often aren't interested in talking about dating/crushes, may not enjoy hypergendered rituals like football games or cheerleading, and might dress in ways that are not typical for our presumed identities. For these reasons, queer folks often are identified as "different" by other students long before they identify that in themselves, and people who are pushed to the margins often are drawn to people who are the same kind of different, even if we don't know exactly why that is.

As part of our internal journeys, many trans folks spend a long time experiencing feelings like gender dysphoria or a desire to be perceived as another identity or have a different body, but because of a lack of representation or inclusive education, we don't have any of the tools to talk about it. Learning about trans and queer identities might *seem* like it's the first step—the opening of the faucet so the water can start running—but more often it's actually the bursting of a dam that's been ready to blow for a while. When one person in a friend group learns these words and shares them with the others, we often see a cascade of breaking dams—dams that would have broken eventually but all happen at once as people learn crucial bits of information at the same time.

A question to reflect on about this concern is: With all the hate that transgender people often face in school and in the world around them, what does someone have to gain by coming out just to follow a trend? Why would someone lie about this?

Fear or Guilt That You Aren't Moving Fast Enough

A lot of people share with me that they're concerned they aren't learning or improving with their support fast enough for their VIP or that their VIP is upset with them for the speed they're going. Whether it's with getting their name and pronouns right or feeling ready to support them coming out to others, you may be feeling like your VIP is frustrated that you aren't on the same page as them right away. (If your fear is about name and pronouns specifically, or about saying the wrong thing, refer back to chapter 1).

First, a reframe: Take a moment to consider the age range of your VIP. Think about a whole group of adjectives you might use to describe people in that age range. I know that I might describe young kids as curious, energetic, kind, and silly. For teens, I might say passionate, intimidating (I'm not ashamed to admit I'm a little afraid of teenagers), and exploratory. There are lots of words you might think of to describe whatever age group your VIP is in, but I'm going to go out on a limb and guess that "patient" was not at the top of the list.

We don't typically think of young people overall as being patient, yet transgender youth are the exception: We're expected to be extremely patient, very well researched, and highly tolerant to hateful opinions regardless of how old we are when we come out. Essentially, we're expected to be more mature than many adults—with the stakes that we won't be supported or respected if we aren't. I would describe myself as an extremely patient person, and I think that in my current line of work it is absolutely a superpower, but I also know that I was forced to become this patient because I felt I wouldn't have been worthy of support from the people around me if I wasn't.

We certainly want to teach our VIPs how to be patient—it's a very helpful and important skill to learn as they mature—but we can't expect them to have the patience of fully developed adults from the moment they come out to us.

In addition to wanting to give your VIP some extra grace, I want you to give *yourself* some grace too. Especially if this is your first close encounter with the trans community, it's okay to acknowledge that there might have to be *a lot* of shifting in the way you view the world. Gender and cisnormativity (defining cisgender as the norm and expectation) have ruled our entire lives, and things like the gender binary and gender roles dominate so many parts of how the world (and especially the United States) operates. It's okay to need to take a minute to adjust to a totally new way of thinking. As long as you are making your best effort to learn and understand, your VIP, as well as most of the trans folks you will meet in life, will likely be appreciative of your effort. Just remember, as I said in chapter 1, the newness of these topics isn't a free pass not to try, it's an acknowledgement that it will take you a combination of time *and* effort.

GROUNDING YOURSELF IN JOY

After reading this chapter, you might have a bit of a heavy feeling on your chest, and we certainly have been talking about some heavy things, but I want to make sure I close this chapter out with some joy and an important reminder: The way you think and talk about things influences how you feel, so don't forget to celebrate! The way we respond to and frame these thoughts in our minds will impact the way we feel about them. The more time we spend dwelling on thoughts that inspire fear, sadness, or anger, the more time we're going to spend sitting in those emotions.

Something my first therapist talked to me about in high school was the idea of metathinking, or thinking about thinking. I thought that every thought that came into my brain should be treated like out-loud speech, where you have to think about and respond to everything someone says to you. She suggested I instead think of my thoughts like paper boats floating down a river. I can't choose whether the boats are in the water—they're there—but I can choose if I want to pick one up out of the stream and inspect it or if I want to just let it float off into the distance. If I pick up every negative thought-boat I see coming down the stream because I feel like I have to acknowledge it, I'm going to end up sitting surrounded by a pile of negative thought-boats and feeling pretty down. Instead, I might notice a negative thought-boat floating and just say to myself, "That's interesting" and let it keep floating away while I reach for more positive or productive thought boats.

This doesn't mean that I think we should ignore every negative thought we have either; it means that *balance* is critical. If you notice there are a lot more negative thought-boats in the stream, it might be time to look for some additional resources for support. We'll discuss this more in the next chapter.

The more you consciously choose to celebrate your VIP's identity with them, the more positive your feelings about their identity are likely to be. Our thoughts impact our feelings, which in turn impact our actions, which impact our thoughts, and so on and so forth, so while you can't control your feelings, remember that you do have control over your thoughts and your actions, and that can help improve your feelings!

6

PROTECTING YOUR VIP'S MENTAL AND EMOTIONAL HEALTH

One of the key worries we discussed in the last chapter is fear for your VIP's safety, and that includes both physical and psychological safety. In this chapter, we're going to talk about mental health, including some of the challenges that may arise for your VIP and the ways you can support them. We're also going to talk about ways you can support your own mental health too, which is just as important.

First, a note of explanation. There is an incorrect association between mental illness and trans identities that many people use to justify a lack of support for the trans community, essentially saying, "If being trans causes so many mental health problems, no one should be trans"—or even worse, "Being trans must be a result of mental illness." It's true that the trans (and overall LGBTQ+) community has a much higher rate of mental health challenges than their cisgender peers, but our thinking about this cause-and-effect relationship is often backward.

The directional relationship that actually exists here is the fact that being trans in a society that does not always support you—where you face harassment and discrimination just for living authentically—is exhausting, and *that* would be enough to cause anxiety or depression in anyone, let alone a young person still learning how to walk through the world and handle day-to-day stressors.

MINORITY STRESS THEORY

If we want to support the mental health of our VIPs, we must address their specific challenges as well as the *causes* of those challenges. Minority stress theory is a model that's been studied for decades and has found concrete evidence that the discrimination, stigma, and judgment faced by members of marginalized groups has measurable impacts on their mental and physical health. In addition to the effects of experienced discrimination, it has been found in multiple studies spanning decades that *anticipated* discrimination has an equally negative effect on the mind and body.[1]

This means that even for someone living in a state with full protections who has supportive friends and family and access to all the resources they need likely knows that in other parts of the country, or even other parts of their own state, there is a target on their back. They're aware of a vague existential threat and might face comments or microaggressions daily that seem small but add up, and this takes a toll on them. In addition to concrete things they might be anxious or depressed about, these daily worries can also evolve into general struggles with anxiety disorders and depressive disorders.

From a language perspective, it's important to note that experiencing the feelings of anxiety or depression is different than having an anxiety disorder or a depressive disorder and your VIP may require different solutions to best support them. While some things might cause feelings of anxiety or depression, in someone with a disorder, these feelings may show up without cause. I have an anxiety disorder, which means that some days I wake up with a looming sense of dread that I can't quite explain. There isn't always an extremely logical cause-effect-solution pathway for negative emotions, but it doesn't mean there's *nothing* you can do; it just means you can't make your VIP feel all better in one conversation and may need to bring in more resources.

ENCOURAGING OPEN CONVERSATION

It is also worth noting that because coming out is often the result of extensive self-reflection, LGBTQ+ people are more likely to notice and identify symptoms of mental illnesses while they are questioning their thoughts and behaviors. I firmly believe that there are many people in the world who struggle with anxiety and depression, but because of how atypical it is culturally for people to speak openly about their feelings, they can't (or don't know that they can) seek support or resources.

Unless you are reading this book from the perspective of a therapist, I'm not going to encourage you to fill the role of a therapist for your VIP, but making sure they know that they can come to you with their feelings, however big or small, will be important in helping them through any potential mental health struggles (Don't worry, we'll talk about therapy in a few pages). There are a variety of ways you can encourage your VIP to share their feelings with you, and it's important that you find a way to do so that feels authentic to your relationship. Here are a few examples:

- Normalize sharing how you are feeling with others and asking for the support that you need (from your VIP specifically or just in front of them to model the language).
  "I'm having an anxious day today; could I have a hug?"
  "I'm feeling really overwhelmed today; I think I need some time on my own."
  "Something really stressful happened at work today; could we talk about it later?"
- Find age-appropriate books to read together about the importance of talking through what you may be feeling. (These are often categorized online as books for social-emotional learning.)
- Be open about your own use of resources to let your VIP know that it is nothing to be ashamed of.
  "I've got therapy at noon today; want to go to lunch afterward?"

THERAPY!

Just like it's normalized to go to the doctor if you break your arm, it should be normalized to see a therapist when you need extra support. I have been in therapy for years and can honestly say it has *dramatically* increased my quality of life.

Therapy is an incredible service that can be so many things for so many people. I can't tell you the specifics of what goes on in therapy, but that's because it can be whatever you need it to be. Different therapists focus on different styles: some focused more on reflection and others more on dialogue, some giving advice and others helping you find your own way to where you need to be. Though there has historically been a lot of stigma surrounding it, going to therapy is not an admission of failure or weakness, just like going to the gym isn't admitting you're weak; in fact, it's admitting that you want to get *even stronger.*

I am a big proponent of breaking down the stigma around therapy, openly sharing with others that I have been in therapy on and off over the course of my transition and that it has changed and saved my life in more ways than I can count. My therapist even had great thoughts to share on the content of this book, as well as many of the stressors that came along with writing it.

There are many new challenges that are going to arise as your VIP begins to walk through the world as a trans person, regardless of their age (though especially if they are younger), and therapy can help them work through those challenges and build the skills to work through them on their own. Therapy is an incredible shield against many of the mental health challenges we discussed earlier in the chapter. In addition, for many transition-related medical procedures, spending at least six months with a therapist (or even two separate therapists) is often a requirement.

Finding the Right Therapist

Finding a suitable therapist can be a process, but it is well worth putting some extra time into the search, as a bad therapist can do a whole lot of damage in a few short sessions. There are a few things you should look for specifically, as well as a few things to look out for as red or yellow flags, in a potential therapist.

There are many websites you can use to find therapists in your area, and therapists can include a list of their focus areas to help people searching for specific resources. Unfortunately, many therapists come at this listing from a marketing angle and add that they can discuss LGBTQ+ issues because they have general knowledge about LGBTQ+ topics, not because they have had any specific training on the unique mental health challenges of the trans and queer community.

There are several ways you can vet potential therapists, and it's important to remember that finding a therapist is about finding the right fit, as your VIP is going to be developing a vulnerable, trusting relationship with this individual. The first step is to try to find reviews from transgender or LGBTQ+ people or get recommendations from local LGBTQ+ centers. Some therapy practices serve as sponsors for LGBTQ+ organizations or have high visibility at LGBTQ+ focused events like pride, and this is a great indicator that they care genuinely and actively about supporting the queer community and are likely to have more knowledge. You also can call therapists' offices directly and share that you're looking for a therapist who has a *focus area* on the transgender community. (It's important to highlight trans or nonbinary, not just LGBTQ+, as the challenges around diverse sexualities can sometimes be very different than those around trans identities.)

Another great way to find a knowledgeable and supportive therapist both for you and your VIP is to find someone who shares the identities you feel are relevant to what you'll be talking about. If you want to talk about the intersection of transness and disability, find a disabled trans therapist. If you want to talk about how it feels to be a nonbinary Muslim, find someone who holds those identities as well. If you're looking for someone who can speak to the intersections of LGBTQ+ identities and race, I highly recommend looking into the National Queer and Trans Therapists of Color Network (NQTTCN).

Because marginalized identities didn't become marginalized by accident, it means we are often left out of the curriculum in master of social work programs (among most other types of programs), and people end up needing to teach their therapists or other healthcare providers about their identities before they can get help with the issues they're facing. I have worked with a lot of different therapists in my life, and they've all been lovely and challenging in different ways, but working with someone who is a member of the LGBTQ+ community means that when I use niche vocabulary words to explain how I'm feeling or talk about the stress around public bathrooms that every gender-nonconforming person knows too well, I don't have to take the time out of my session to define and explain those terms and topics to my therapist because they already understand it. When they ask me insightful questions, it's generally not to make sure they know what I'm talking about but to help me think through new perspectives on a much deeper level.

Quality of Therapy Strategies

There are also a few different approaches therapists may take when talking to trans people, especially trans young people: one focused on affirmation, one focused on investigation, and one focused on "alternative solutions."

Therapists focused on affirmation take your VIP's words about their identity as the truth. They ask plenty of insightful questions and provide them a safe space to explore and question their identity without judgment or withdrawal of support, and they are consistent about honoring the chosen name and pronouns of your VIP. They also focus more on supporting the VIP in the areas that they're struggling with and generally are less interested in what might be "causing them" to have their identity. I would highly recommend finding an affirming therapist for your VIP, and while in the process of vetting therapists you can ask what their stance is on affirming the identity of their clients.

Therapists focused on investigation have the goal of making sure your VIP is "really trans." This is not necessarily malicious in intent, but the impact can be harmful. With investigative therapists, there will be a lot more focus on "but have you considered that what you might actually be feeling is xyz?" This is going to send the message to your VIP that this therapist—and by association, you, if you were involved in their selection—does not want them to be trans and is working toward finding a way out. It also creates a space where trans people can't share any doubts or questions about their identity because it may create an opening for the therapist to withdraw support for your VIP in their identity. Recently, this type of therapy has been dubbed "Gender Exploratory Therapy" but is typically just conversion therapy by another name.

There are also therapists who are explicitly focused on making people not transgender, though they'll usually use other words like "alternative solutions for gender dysphoria." They are often, but not always, religious, and they work through a process called "conversion therapy," which attempts to change the sexual orientation or gender identity of their clients. Activists are fighting tirelessly to get conversion therapy banned, as it has been clearly shown by years of research to have no effects outside of immense psychological damage.

Inpatient Treatment

While I wish I could say that with supportive allies and a good therapist, all your VIP's mental health issues will resolve themselves, the reality is that for many people, mental illness is an ongoing battle, with some days more victorious than others. I hate that we need to talk about this, but the tragic reality is that there are higher rates of eating disorders, self-harm, and suicidal ideation among trans youth, and it's important to be aware of this. While being surrounded by support is a protective factor, there are many things you can't always control—other students at school, political attacks, dysphoria, isolation, and other factors can be a huge weight on your VIP's shoulders.

Sometimes your VIP may need more support than you're able to give. This isn't due to any failing on your part; sometimes things come up that require professional support. If you have concerns about your VIP's immediate safety, it may be wise to seek out an inpatient psychiatry program. It is extremely important as you go through this process that you take the time to find a program that is explicitly trans affirming. While it might feel like the most important thing is to get somewhere *now*, spending any amount of time in a program that refuses to see your VIP as they are will likely end up doing more harm than good.

PROTECTING AGAINST "DESIGNATED EDUCATOR" BURNOUT

Once the wheels begin to turn on the public coming-out process, it is likely your VIP will start to receive quite a few questions. As we discussed in chapter 3, it can be tiring to have to answer an endless list of questions around our identities and personal experiences, and this is especially true for young people early in the coming-out process. When I came out, I was thrown headfirst into the role of question answering with all my classmates, and it was so exciting. Every day, I spoke with people who had never met a transgender person before or just wanted to become better allies, shared my story, and answered their questions. I freely shared my knowledge, my experiences, my struggles, and my patience in answering lists of mostly benign but occasionally invasive or inappropriate questions. For months I gave everything I could to every person who came to me, but all that giving started to catch up to me as I realized that even if the conversation went great, I always left a bit more tired than I was before.

By the time I graduated high school, I had decided I was going to never tell anyone I was trans ever again, just so I didn't have to be "that trans guy" anymore. There were a few things that made this time of my life so specifically exhausting.

First were the stakes. Because most people I spoke with were new to learning about the transgender community, each conversation felt like a mental battle to try to convince them that my community was real and deserved acceptance. It was stressful right out of the gate because I knew if I wasn't patient enough or didn't answer enough questions the right way, the people I talked to may not support me through my transition. (Some of this was my own perception, but other times I was told that directly.) Once I realized there were more transgender people coming out after me who would also have to fight for that acceptance, my stress grew exponentially. If I was too tired to answer someone's question, would they direct their confusion, hesitance, or anger at the next trans person they met? With that driving force constantly on the back of my mind, I upheld a personal policy of answering every single question that came my way, regardless of what I wanted or needed at that time.

Second was learning very quickly that most social rules and boundaries didn't seem to apply to trans people. People felt entitled to know about every intimate detail of my body, my sexuality, my surgical plans, and other things an adult would otherwise never dream of asking a child (or another adult, for that matter). Navigating those conversations was always challenging, and I didn't have the language or confidence to simply say, "That question makes me uncomfortable and I'd rather not answer it."

Third was feeling like I had to be an expert, which fifteen-year-olds are historically not known to be. I knew I had to be a perfect representation of my community and be prepared to answer every question about my identity and the broader LGBTQ+ community, and I had no one to ask and nowhere to turn to get answers to my own questions.

Carrying the weight of being a perfect educator was certainly draining, but there was also something special about it. I knew that I was making an impact and I enjoyed feeling like I was good at something. Your VIP might love answering questions or they might hate it; what's key to understand is that this weight will exist either way. Whether or not someone enjoys these conversations or even seeks them out doesn't change the fact that these exchanges involve a whole lot of giving. The energy and time given to them has to come from somewhere, and at some point it can and will run out.

It will likely take me a lifetime to be able to develop a full understanding of how to lay down boundaries and recharge my educator batteries, but I've developed a few methods of self-preservation that may be helpful for you and your VIP to discuss.

Finding or Creating Question-Free Spaces

Because of how much of my day-to-day life and work revolve around answering questions, one of the most important things for my own mental health is being present in spaces where I know I'm not going to be asked any questions: no definitions, no defenses of my own humanity, nothing. For me, this exists in LGBTQ+ affinity spaces like book clubs and social events, but I also find this around my family and close friends, with whom I've shared the ways that answering questions can be draining. This doesn't mean my LGBTQ+ and ally friends aren't allowed to ask me questions; they just are conscious of picking the right time and place for it and prefacing it with, "Hey Ben, whenever you're up for it, I've got a question I'd love to get your thoughts on." Helping your VIP find these spaces may look like helping introduce them to an LGBTQ+ club or support group or establishing times in your house that are just for playing board games, having fun, and not talking about any of the nuances of gender identity.

Capacity Planning

Early in my career as a public speaker, my schedule was jam-packed every day. Running between meetings, tasks, and virtual speeches all day left me feeling drained, and I assumed this was simply how it felt to be a working professional. Though it's true that working full time can be exhausting, I've found that how I arrange my schedule can make a significant difference in my energy at the end of the day. Though by and large my schedule looks even busier now than it did when I started working, there's one major difference in my calendar: On days when I'm giving a presentation, my afternoon is otherwise empty. Since late 2021, I've been practicing what's known as "capacity planning," where I think through each of my meetings, tasks, and speeches for a week and make notes on those I anticipate will be more draining. On days when I give a speech—which is by far one of the most tiring (and still most fun) things I do—I spend the rest of the day reading books with queer characters, walking my dog, talking on the phone with friends, or catching up on my favorite TV show. I've identified which of my metaphorical batteries the speech will drain and planned a day of pre- and post-speech recharge that significantly lowers any emotional toll it may have on me.

This is an extremely useful skill to practice with your VIP, and it may come up around coming-out conversations, spaces where they have to hear their birth name often, or times when they are stepping into a planned or unplanned educator role. Helping them to check in with themselves after different conversations and events to ask how they're feeling and what they'd like to do next, as well as modeling conservations around your own capacity planning, can help them build this into their toolkit.

It's important to acknowledge as well that predictions may not be 100 percent correct. There are times when I leave a typically normal one-on-one call feeling totally drained, and times where I leave a speech feeling like I'm on top of the world and *almost* could go for a run (though if you do see me actually running, it's likely because someone is chasing me and not because I'm in a good mood). There may be times when your VIP needs to leave an event early or cancel other plans because something took a lot out of them, or they may have more energy than you expected them to, so check in regularly and follow their lead.

Setting Storytelling Boundaries

Like any person, I have a wide variety of experiences—good and bad—that I draw from to tell stories and emphasize points. In conversations and speeches about my identity, I used to share the most personal stories I had, which were also some of my most painful memories. These were and still are challenging stories to tell, and I reached a point where I decided that any benefit my audience might receive from hearing those stories didn't outweigh the detriment to my own mental health, and that I could have the same effect with stories that were not nearly as private. I also came to the slow realization that most conversations are an *exchange* in which individuals earn each other's trust and share personal things, and the folks I was giving presentations to had not earned the level of trust required to talk about my darkest moments.

I see a hunger for trans stories all around me, and unfortunately a lot of that hunger is focused on pain and trauma. Not only are there people who want to hear about our worst moments or our most transphobic encounters, but some people even feel entitled to those stories and frustrated when we are not willing to share them. While giving a speech, I once had someone casually ask me, "What's the worst thing that's ever happened to you?" as if that were a perfectly normal question to ask another person.

As your VIP thinks through which of their own stories they want to share and how they want to share them, encourage them to decide if there are any stories they want to hold as "just for them," or stories that only come up in more personal, trusting conversations. I know sometimes it can feel like the worst stories are the ones that provoke the strongest feelings of empathy, but I've also found that what people are really looking for is any kind of strong emotion. I can get the same empathetic response from telling a powerfully joyful story as I can from a deeply painful story, and I get to feel much better after I tell it! (In case you couldn't tell by now, centering joy is kind of my "thing.")

Saying No

One of the biggest—if not *the* biggest—skills that any person can develop in life is the ability to confidently say "no." For trans people, developing this skill is particularly crucial for navigating the variety of personal questions we may be asked. Because different people have different personality types and styles of communication, there's no one right way to say you're not interested in answering a question, so what matters is helping your VIP find a way to answer that feels authentic to them. For me, I will either explain why a question isn't appropriate to ask, point the questioner toward a resource where they can get the answer, or try to deflect with humor. Others may just say they aren't comfortable or ask someone else to step in to help. With time and practice, your VIP will find the way that feels the most comfortable for them, but know that there may be times you might need to step in to help them enforce that "no."

SUPPORTING YOUR VIP THROUGH GENDER DYSPHORIA

The mental health challenges we've explored so far are not necessarily specific to the trans community, though they're often exacerbated by trans experiences. Now I also want to talk for a moment about feelings of dysphoria and ways you might be able to support your VIP through times where dysphoria is more present and painful. As with any other tip I give, it's very important to talk to your VIP about what helps *them* the most, but this section will give you some starting points.

In general, dysphoria can be broken down into social dysphoria and physical dysphoria. On a fundamental level, social dysphoria is the pain of not being seen by others as you see yourself. Being misgendered, feeling like an outsider, or facing transphobia in general are some likely culprits of social dysphoria. Here are some things you can do to help alleviate social dysphoria:

- Help your VIP pick hairstyles or outfits that may help them be more frequently gendered correctly (while also following their lead and not forcing them to make any changes they don't want to).
- Agree on code words your VIP can use to let you know that they'd like you to intervene or that they'd like to leave a social setting because they're uncomfortable.
- Keep track of the number of times your VIP is misgendered in a day and having "prizes" for passing certain thresholds. Getting misgendered fifteen times doesn't sound quite as bad when it comes with a double scoop in a waffle cone!
- Ensure you are finding community spaces (we'll talk more about this in the next chapter) where your VIP knows they will be seen as they are.
- Over-index on using their correct name and pronouns as well as gendered words that they feel comfortable with, like "handsome" or "daughter," to counter the impact of the incorrect words used by others.

- Join them in things that make them feel comfortable so they don't feel like they're an outsider. I always felt embarrassed needing to wear a swim shirt to the pool, for example, but having friends who wore one too meant I didn't feel as alone in it.
- Play a game in which you refer to them as an undercover agent, with their old name and pronouns as their false identity for the purpose of the mission. This may sound silly, but "going undercover" got me through countless school days and family functions before I was able to come out.

Physical dysphoria can be a little harder to deal with because it isn't necessarily caused by an external force. If I were alone on a desert island, I would still experience physical dysphoria. There are parts of my body I was very uncomfortable with, and I avoided, as much as possible, anything that made me aware of those body parts. Even now I have days where some parts of my body just don't feel right. While medical transition, which we'll talk about in chapter 8, is one option to mitigate physical dysphoria, it is not instantly accessible, nor is it necessarily what everyone wants. Here are a few suggestions for ways you can mitigate physical dysphoria outside of a medical setting:

- Purchase a dim nightlight or LED light for the bathroom or shower. Early in my transition, I often showered with the lights off to avoid needing to see my body, though as you can likely imagine, showering in pitch darkness came with its own set of challenges. Sometimes it also helped to shower in a swim shirt or T-shirt.
- Support your VIP in purchasing appropriately sized gender-affirming shapewear like chest binders, TransTape, or tucking underwear, which help safely minimize parts of the body that trans folks may be uncomfortable with.
- Support them in getting haircuts that make them feel affirmed, as well as in purchasing clothes that emphasize the traits they enjoy or the ones they want. I often wore thick button-down shirts and sweaters because they created a much less "curvy" look and helped to minimize my chest. There are also many clothing brands specifically designed for trans bodies.

- Mirror the language your VIP uses to talk about their body. For example, I always use the word "chest" instead of "breasts" because it feels more gender-neutral to me. As long as you are both on the same page about what you're referring to, it's okay to not use the precise anatomical terminology.

- If your VIP is struggling with specific things about their body—for example, facial hair, a deep voice, or small hands—help them find examples of cisgender celebrities or other people they admire who have those traits. Biological sex is not nearly as binary as we like to think, and reminding your VIP that some men have small feet and some women have mustaches can be a great affirmation.

- If appropriate, have a conversation with your VIP about which parts of their body bring them dysphoria and avoid situations or items of clothing that might draw attention to those body parts.

Of course, I'd be remiss if I didn't share one of my favorite (and, frankly, one of the funniest) dysphoria-reducing armors: a giant hoodie. What better way to avoid thinking about your body than by wearing a piece of clothing so oversized that you can't tell a thing about the body underneath? This may sound funny, but thick fabric that doesn't do any sort of body-contouring can be very helpful in reducing dysphoria as it comes up. While trans experiences are not a monolith, almost every trans person I know has at least one giant emotional support hoodie.

SOCIAL MEDIA USE

Social media and online news outlets are a powerful tool for finding community, connection, and information, but it can sometimes feel like drinking from a firehose of bad news. While we have access to news and information 24/7, just because we *can* does not always mean we *should* be checking the news at all times.

It can be very easy to feel guilty for not staying as informed as possible, for not spending time engaging with every post about the latest tragedy or piece of anti-trans legislation, but we aren't built to withstand a torrent of bad news every second of the day. It's important to put in place social media boundaries that help us find space and peace while still staying informed. I would encourage both you and your VIP to find and set social media and general news boundaries that help you feel more grounded.

"Doomscrolling"—scrolling mindlessly through social media while experiencing building existential dread—is a concept many of us are familiar with and is often a numbing behavior. When I realized I had been spending a lot of time doomscrolling on social media, always feeling worse afterward, I decided to set boundaries that would help me avoid those situations. To help you and your VIP create your own boundaries, here are the systems I've set up for myself.

On Staying informed

Unless there's a specific event I'm following, I check the news twice per day: once around 11am, and once around 3pm—never too close to the start of my day, to avoid setting my morning off on the wrong foot, and never too close to the end of my day, to avoid ruining my sleep. When I check the news, I set a timer for ten to fifteen minutes, read stories that tell me things I don't already know, then close the website when the timer is done.

On Comments

As a rule, internet comment sections are never productive. They're the domain of of trolls, bad faith arguments, and immediate escalation. Responding to hateful comments might feel good in the moment, but it's rarely going to be productive and usually just saps your emotional energy (and your time). I avoid comments sections as much as humanly possible. (If you really want to respond, we'll talk more about when and how to do so in chapter 10.)

On New Information

Many news articles tell me things I already know. Not specifically, of course—I can't read the future (at least not yet)—but in general, many articles about trans issues are simply highlighting how cruel people are toward trans people. I want to stay informed, but I can't survive hearing over and over again how much people want to see my community erased, and I already

MY CHILD IS TRANS, NOW WHAT?

know they do, so I will often read the headline or skim for key points and not read all the gory details. This doesn't mean I skip every piece of news I don't want to hear. I want to stay informed, but sometimes I have to acknowledge that I know what the overall message of the article is and don't need to be reminded of that. I try to focus as much as possible on local news to get information that is the most relevant and actionable to me.

On Social Media Exit Codes

It can be overwhelming to see post after post featuring clips of legislative hearings or mentions of general transphobia and homophobia, so I have "exit codes" for social media. If I see more than three videos talking about legislation, I get off whatever app I'm on. If I see just one video about threats of violence or certain other heavy topics that are really challenging for me, I'm off right away. Having preset numbers makes it much easier than just waiting until I notice that I'm totally drained from reading or watching dozens of upsetting stories.

On Intention

A big one for me has been trying to be intentional about the things I do, especially my social media use. Social media isn't an inherently harmful thing, it just has the ability to *become* harmful based on the ways we use it, and for me one of the biggest harms was coming from mindless scrolling. So now, any time I'm about to look at my phone, I stop and ask myself what I am hoping to find on there. Is it connection? Comedy? Information? Meaning? Peace? Then I ask myself if I am 100 percent certain—or even 75 percent certain—that by opening that app I'm guaranteed to find what I'm looking for. When the answer is inevitably "no," I ask myself where I can go to find that 100 percent guarantee: maybe by calling a friend or watching a favorite TV show instead.

On Barriers to Access

I know barriers to access usually indicates something negative, but in this case it's a helpful strategy of just making it a little bit harder to get on to social media. For me, this means deleting the apps off my phone and logging out of websites on my computer when I'm done. Adding that little bit of friction gives me a moment to think about what I'm doing before I do it, and usually in that moment I decide it's not worth it and find something else to do. This is especially helpful in the evenings, when the temptation to check the news or social media is especially strong (and especially negative, with its impacts on the body and sleep).

Everyone uses social media in different ways and will want to set different boundaries, but it's important to make sure you're aware of the mental health costs of certain types of news and media intake, for both your VIP and yourself.

While it's important to talk about safety and boundaries with social media, it's also important to acknowledge the important role social media can play in building community and sharing positive representation. From a community perspective, not everyone lives in a major metropolitan area or a city with an active queer support group. Not everyone can safely search publicly for queer community. Social media can be an incredible resource, but like any other tool, it's important to learn how to use it wisely and safely. If appropriate and relevant, make sure that you're having conversations with your VIP about online privacy and safety best practices.

You aren't going to be able to protect your VIP from every challenge that comes up, and that can be a really hard truth to face. Rather than protect them from everything the world might throw at them, your job is to help prepare them with the skills they'll need to protect themselves from life's inevitable challenges and to be a support system they can lean on whenever they need you.

The good news is that neither you nor your VIP is in this alone, however it might feel in this moment, and in the next chapter we're going to talk more about how to find and lean on a wide variety of community resources to support both of you through all the parts of this journey.

7

FINDING AND LEANING ON YOUR COMMUNITY

Where to Find Support

As I was going through my coming-out journey, one of the reasons I felt so scared was that I felt like I was blazing a new trail, proudly and anxiously wearing the badge of "one of the first trans people in my town." Now I realize how statistically unlikely that was. Though significant efforts have been made to remove transgender people from history books, we know that transgender people have existed for thousands of years. I might have been the second person to come out in my school, but more likely I was just the second person *that I knew of*, and there were likely countless others before me who were trans and weren't able to come out.

As we talked about before, one reason that we feel safe getting on roller coasters is that we've seen so many people get on scared and get off smiling. We know it's scary, but it's established and well researched and *someone else did it first.* You and your VIP are not the first people to go through this, and you're likely not even the only people to be doing it right now in your local community. This is why it's crucial to lean on the resources and community groups around you—feeling less alone, being around people who know exactly what you're going through and may know how to help you is crucial in counteracting many of the challenges that we talked about in the previous two chapters.

In general, resources fall into one (or more) of the following categories:

1. Tactical Support
2. Emotional Support
3. Education
4. Political Action
5. Celebration/Social

Your local LGBTQ+ resource center will likely be a hub for resources in all five categories, and they are very likely to have some sort of directory of available resources in your community. In general, if you're struggling with something relating to your VIP's identity or experience, it's very likely someone else has too and has put together a resource for it, so it's always worth looking.

If you don't have a local LGBTQ+ resource center, look for statewide support organizations, then look to national resources. In general, I recommend a bull's-eye approach: The more local you can get, the better, because large organizations are pulled in many directions and receive thousands of calls for support per day (though are absolutely still worth calling if they're your best option), while local organizations are entirely focused on helping you specifically as a member of their community and will have resources specific to where you are geographically.

Let's talk through some great examples of different kinds of support and how to find them—or start them!

TACTICAL SUPPORT

Tactical support may be one of the most obvious types of resources. Tactical support helps you do things.

Resources in this category may give you information about structural challenges and what you need to do to overcome them. As an example, in some places you may need a lawyer to represent you to get your name legally changed—a costly, time-consuming, and stressful process. Enter the Name Change Project, an organization that helps pair trans folks with lawyers to help them change their legal names and gender markers at little or no cost.

Another of my favorite tactical resources is Strands for Trans, an online resource where trans-affirming barbershops and hair salons can identify themselves as welcoming spaces.

Here is a list of other examples of tactical resources:

- Supportive doctors' offices (general)
- Transgender-specific medical centers
- Legal name change organizations
- Organizations that help families of trans youth flee states with unsupportive laws
- Legal aid for discrimination or similar cases

Because tactical resources often work together on initiatives to support the trans community, they also are likely able to share other resources with you. If you have a connection to a doctor's office or a legal name change group, they are very likely to be able to point you toward other resources that they have partnerships with.

EMOTIONAL SUPPORT

Emotional support, especially from a group of people experiencing something similar to you, can be such a powerful tool for getting guidance and peace during stressful times. There are so many support group options for LGBTQ+ people, and at a variety of intersections as well: There are groups specifically set up to talk about what it's like to be a trans woman, or a trans person of color, or a disabled trans person, or all three! Thanks to the normalization of Zoom and online spaces, you can access these groups via the internet no matter where you live.

There is a good chance your VIP may resist attending a group for a variety of reasons, and I would encourage you to sit with them and talk to them about why they're nervous about it and provide them the information and support to go when they're ready. I, for example, really didn't want to go to my college's Gender and Sexuality Center—not because there was anything wrong with the GSC, but I didn't want to "meet people whose whole personality revolved around being trans." I had spent years in high school being seen only as a trans person, and I couldn't bear the thought that in these spaces other people would see me the same way. In hindsight, I wish I had gone. I experienced a number of challenges on campus that someone there likely would also have gone through and been prepared to support me with. You aren't going to be able to force your VIP to go to a group, but I would recommend strongly encouraging them to.

In addition to your VIP, it can be a fantastic idea for you to go to a support group as well! There are countless organizations set up specifically to help you through this journey. While it's amazing to go to spaces like pride parades and other celebratory events together with your VIP, separate support groups allow you more space to talk about things you're going through and to be in closed spaces with *only* other people who are going through similar things as you. This fits in nicely with ring theory, which we talked about in chapter 5 as the guiding philosophy that there are certain thoughts or feelings that are going to do more harm than good when shared with your VIP. Sharing these thoughts with your VIP present, even if you share afterward that you're feeling better about it, may leave them with doubts or concerns that you still feel that way or that you don't really support them. In a private support group for family members (or teachers, or doctors, or whatever your lens may be), you'll be able to share your thoughts and fears with people who have felt—and gotten through—similar things, which will help you resolve them for yourself.

Some of my personal favorites that have a national presence are PFLAG, Transparent, the Mama Bears, and He, She, Ze, and We. Each of these groups has a website or social media to help you find local groups. You can also look up online "Parents of LGBTQ+ youth support group (insert city name here)" or join a virtual group. If you aren't sure how to find those resources, local LGBTQ+ centers, public libraries, supportive doctors, therapists, religious congregations, or other supportive organizations may be able to point you in the right direction. There are also a number of national and local Facebook groups that you can join to connect with an online community in between real-time group meetings.

With support groups, as well as the other resources we'll discuss later, it's important to do some vetting, as some are run by individuals with nefarious motives (or great motives and terrible execution). Here are the major red flags to look out for in support groups for parents, family members, or other allies to the LGBTQ+ community:

1. Groups focused on "changing someone's mind." It is very rare for an anti-trans group to brand itself as an anti-trans group. They much prefer the terms "gender critical" or "religious liberty." Insidious support groups often have a heavy religious focus and claim to be about loving and supporting your child but actually focus on how to "love the sinner, not the sin" and bring someone "back into the light."

2. Groups that involve a lot of stewing/venting. I know this might sound good in theory, but I have seen groups—particularly in online spaces, but in person as well—where parents come in and share that their child came out as trans and ask a few questions, then are met with a flood of messages reading, "I know this is really hard; here's why else it's so hard" and endless egging-on and commiserating about the challenges associated with having a transgender loved one. These extremely negative groups encourage parents to focus on their grief "as long as they need"—almost always prolonging it significantly—and rarely provide resources or alternative thought patterns to challenge beliefs or misconceptions that parents come in with. The more time you spend around people who just want to talk about how miserable an experience it is, the more you're going to feel like it's a miserable experience too. You should absolutely be allowed to talk about the difficult parts, but in some groups it is the main or only focus, and those should be avoided.

EDUCATION

In addition to receiving support, there are so many things to learn about trans and queer identities, histories, and issues, and it can be extremely impactful to seek both support and education for you and your VIP.

Informative documentaries and TV shows, which may teach you new definitions and teach you about queer history, helping you remember that you are not alone in this moment in time or a part of any trend, are an excellent educational resource. Most importantly, inclusive media can showcase a wide variety of what it can look like to be any number of identities. With the limited knowledge many of us have about different trans identities, it can be easy to boil them down into stereotypes and expect (or even force) trans people to fit into those buckets, but seeing a more feminine trans man, or a trans woman who keeps her facial hair, or a nonbinary person without colored hair can help us break down these stereotypes. It will help you as an ally not make assumptions about what your VIP's journey will have to look like, and it will help your VIP know that their identity can look however they want it to. Consuming media with trans and queer characters with your VIP is also a great way to signal to them that their identity is worth celebrating and talking about, not something shameful that needs to be hidden.

Educational resources can also look like webinars, panels, or discussions at conferences with tactical information about how to go through a legal name change, what a medical transition might entail, or other information about the elements of a transition. There are a wide variety of conferences that create educational spaces for transgender people and those who support them, often put on by the national organizations behind some of the support groups we spoke about earlier, like PFLAG or Free Mom Hugs.

This chapter is particularly "meta," as the kids would say—writing about educational resources *in* an educational resource. Books and support guides like this one fall into the educational resource category as well!

POLITICAL ACTION

Next up is political action resources. This includes resources that inform you what your VIP's rights are in your state, town, or school, as well as legal resources that will support you should someone try to infringe on those rights.

This also includes organizations fighting to support your VIP's rights on a state and national level. Whether you want to get involved in politics or not, the reality is that politics wants to get involved with you. As I sit here writing this section in early 2023, four hundred anti-trans bills have been proposed across the United States, targeting everyone from parents to athletes to doctors to teachers, and "not getting political" isn't going to stop those bills from passing.

What does stop these bills is the incredible work of organizations like the ACLU, the Trevor Project, the Equality Federation, and many other national, state, and local organizations, as well as the passionate work of individual trans people and allies willing to go to bat for us. Neither you nor your VIP has to get involved in politics (although we'll talk more thoroughly in later chapters about how to get involved if you wish), but it's important to be prepared and know what resources exist in your area so that if a problem arises, you are ready to tackle it.

CELEBRATION AND SOCIAL RESOURCES

Our goal in finding people and resources to connect to is not entirely utilitarian. As humans, we are naturally social creatures who want to spend time around other people for enjoyment. Having a community of people who make you feel safe, seen, and loved is so crucial for anyone, and it's important for both you and your VIP to spend time in social and celebratory spaces where you can just focus on being a human and having a good time.

Social events include things like movie nights and game nights—not things that necessarily need to be LGBTQ+ focused at all. Just being in a group of people who you know have no interest in debating your VIP's right to exist can be extremely relaxing. If you're a member of any other types of resource groups, consider adding a once-a-month casual hangout to your calendar or reaching out to other parents of trans youth to spend social time together.

Celebratory events are often larger, although they certainly don't have to be, and are moments when your VIP can see just how loved they are. Events like pride parades or LGBTQ+ history festivals send a message of love and support and allow your VIP to be in a group of people that not only tolerates and accepts them, but is *delighted* by their presence. Going to celebratory events with your VIP is a great way to show that you feel their identity is worth celebrating—a message you should send as often as you possibly can. It is also a great way to continue normalizing LGBTQ+ identities and expressions for yourself, as pride parades are truly a time for everyone to come out and be themselves.

Realistically, you aren't going to have a different group for each of these buckets, neatly divided and compartmentalized. These categories are going to overlap and intertwine, and the same group might fill multiple purposes for you. The important point is that there are so many types of resources available based on what you need, and you shouldn't try to go on this journey alone. It is not a failing of any kind to seek support or resources, it does not imply that you are not "enough" to support your VIP. It simply means that you don't need to reinvent the wheel and that you and your VIP deserve to be supported and reminded that you are not alone.

Though it may be hard to find at first, the community of LGBTQ+ people and their allies is present everywhere, however loud or quiet they may be in specific areas, and leaning on them is crucial to finding joy and peace on this journey.

8

MEDICAL TRANSITION

It's time to jump into another hot topic: medical transition. While we'll talk about the landscape of healthcare overall in a chapter 12, for now I want to focus on transition-specific medical procedures. I'm going to briefly touch on what the most common medical procedures are so you understand them as they come up in conversations with your VIP and others, but I am not going to go into depth about them. The reality is that I'm not the person you should be learning about this from, and it isn't just because I'm not a doctor (though that's part of it).

Even if I were the leading medical expert on gender transition procedures, I could not write a book that would tell you or your VIP what to do and what that experience will look like. That is the job of *your VIP's doctor*. Different people want different things, different surgeries will look differently on different bodies, hormone therapy will have different effects on different people, and a good doctor can come up with a plan to address their patient's specific needs and meet their specific goals. Additionally, new studies are released every day with additional information about these procedures and their effects, and a review of the most up-to-date literature as of this writing might be old news by the time you pick this book up.

In short, this chapter cannot replace a conversation with your VIP's doctor. Instead, it should be used as a tool to supplement that conversation, address any misconceptions or fears, and share the language and details around the most common procedures.

MEDICAL MYTH BUSTING

As one of the current major political targets, there is a lot of misinformation around gender-affirming care. In chapter 10, we'll discuss misinformation as a whole, but to start us off here I'm going to break down some of the most common myths and share some important reminders about transition-related and gender-affirming care:

- *MYTH:* All transgender people have a goal of "completing" their transition and having every surgery possible.
  FACT: Not every trans person wants to medically transition. Different people want different things, or no things at all, at different times, and there is no one "right" path that someone must take. Transition is not a staircase where you climb a series of ordered medical steps to hit the goal of "completing the transition." The goal is just to get you where you want to be at that time in your life. For years, I wasn't particularly interested in going on hormone replacement therapy (HRT) and people constantly asked me when I was going to "finish my transition" or who was stopping me from going on hormones. They assumed that I was following the only path they'd heard of, and they weren't able to hear me when I tried to share with them that I wasn't interested in it. When they did hear me, they interpreted it as my saying I wasn't certain about my trans identity, which had nothing to do with my decision relating to hormones.
- *MYTH:* Transgender people need to medically transition because they are miserable without it.
  FACT: Misery is not the only factor that drives a person's decision to go through medical changes, and although conversations of dysphoria dominated the conversation about trans people for a long time, our goal should be to help trans folks feel at home in their bodies instead of just "not miserable." Gender euphoria is an equally important driving factor in why someone might want to go through certain changes. When I

eventually decided to start hormones, it was after careful consideration and talking with my doctor about some of the misconceptions I had about the changes I would see. With extensive research, I realized that even if I wasn't miserable without hormones, I could be *even happier* with hormones, and I decided to start HRT.

- *MYTH:* Gender-affirming care was invented for trans people.

  FACT: Gender affirming care isn't just for trans people! Anything someone might do that makes them feel more "like a man" or "like a woman" is gender-affirming care. Cis men can buy testosterone and hair growth supplements at the grocery store. Most breast augmentations are done on cis women, not trans women. Botox, HRT for folks in menopause, surgery for gynecomastia (men with breasts), and Viagra are just a few examples of the many different types of gender-affirming care.

- *MYTH:* Gender-affirming care is new and dangerous.

  FACT: Many, if not all, of these treatments have been used for decades for a variety of purposes, including transition-related care, and are very well researched and firmly established as safe when done with a trusted healthcare provider. Puberty blockers, for example, have been used for more than forty years to treat young cisgender people who start puberty too early.

- *MYTH:* Gender-affirming care is experimental treatment with no regulation.

  FACT: Gender-affirming care is carefully observed, regulated, and researched. On a global level, the World Professional Association for Transgender Health (WPATH) has been around for decades creating helpful and informative documents about best-practice standards of care for transgender people of all ages. Its most recent document, the Standards of Care 8, took thirteen years to develop and contains more than two hundred pages of research and recommendations.

- *MYTH:* There's so little research about gender-affirming care and hormone therapy.

  FACT: There is currently a very large body of research that is expanding rapidly as additional studies are published, nearly all of them drawing the same conclusions about the low risks and high mental health benefits of gender-affirming care. Historically, there also used to be significantly more research. In the 1920s and 1930s, a German

man by the name of Magnus Hirschfeld ran the Institute for Sexual Research, which performed gender-affirming surgeries, provided hormone replacement therapy, shared sex education, and did substantial research.[1] With the rise of the Nazi regime, the institute was burned, destroying twenty thousand irreplaceable books and all but erasing it from history.

- *MYTH:* Anyone can get gender-affirming care at the drop of a hat. *FACT:* Gender-affirming care is not something that people have access to immediately after coming out. There are many barriers to accessing gender-affirming care, including extremely long wait times and paperwork requirements that include multiple letters from different therapists "proving" our identities and need for care. No one is going on HRT mere days after they come out to themselves.

YOUTH MEDICAL TRANSITION

To go a bit deeper about a specifically contentious topic, I want to talk about the nebulous cloud of fear and misinformation surrounding the thought of kids transitioning. There is a misconception that when a young person, especially someone under thirteen, comes out as transgender, they immediately get surgery or go on hormones. This misconception is often pushed as a way to scare people into supporting anti-trans healthcare bans and even goes so far as to encourage extremists to call in threats to hospitals that provide care for transgender youth.

To dispel some of those misconceptions, let's take a look at what transition and medical transition look like at young ages (specifically before puberty).

When we talk about transition or gender exploration before puberty, we almost always exclusively mean social transition. They may want to change their hair, their clothes, their name, or their pronouns, but there are no doctors doing gender-transition-related surgeries on anyone before puberty.[2]

As a child gets older, they may start what is referred to as "puberty blockers," which act as a pause button on puberty, giving young people a chance to think a bit longer about whether they'd like to go on HRT or whether they'd like to go through the puberty of the sex they were assigned at birth.

Puberty blockers prevent things like breast growth, voice deepening, and facial hair growth, allowing young trans people time to make sure they know what they'd like to do without having the ticking clock of the appearance of hard-to-reverse effects of puberty.

One of the main claims of the current phase of anti-trans bills is that people should just be able to wait until they're eighteen to go on hormones or make any permanent changes to their bodies. It's true that hormones do make some changes that are permanent and some that are reversible—and that's *all* hormones, not just external hormone replacement therapy. When young people are forced to go through the wrong puberty, permanent changes happen to them that they will spend a lifetime trying to undo or make peace with. As a personal example, I was absolutely miserable with the ways my body changed during puberty. I eventually had top surgery, but if I had been on puberty blockers I wouldn't have needed it because my body wouldn't have grown in those ways in the first place.

As a broader example, bone structure, which impacts height, shoulder broadness, jawline, hand size, and shoe size (among other things), is deeply dependent on hormones and is mostly set between the ages of sixteen and eighteen. With puberty blockers, trans women are less likely to grow taller and broader shouldered, and with hormone therapy trans men will grow to a more typical male height. Both will also have much more "naturally" feminine- or masculine-sounding voices. Waiting until they're eighteen means that medical transition procedures are more likely to focus on undoing the damage of having gone through the wrong puberty rather than going through the correct puberty the first time.

If you have specific concerns about the impacts of hormone blockers on your VIP, there are many doctors and transgender health centers that focus specifically on providing world-class, well-researched medical care to trans youth that would be happy to talk through your specific concerns with you.

COMMON SURGERIES

Now let's walk through some of the most common treatments and procedures so you will have the tools to learn what these procedures mean to your VIP and can ask informed questions of your VIP's healthcare provider.

Remember, not everyone is going to want to have every procedure on this list. This isn't a five-course meal with planned dishes in stages; it's a buffet where folks can take as much or as little as they'd like.

You may notice that I've broken the surgeries out into AFAB (assigned female at birth) and AMAB (assigned male at birth) rather than trans men and trans women. This is because those who identify outside the gender binary also sometimes go through medical changes, and as such, I've sorted the surgeries into the types of bodies they are performed on rather than the identities of the people having the procedures. To give you the most up-to-date information on these processes and procedures, I'm be pulling information from UCSF's Transgender Care information page as well as from my own personal experiences and those of other trans folks.[3]

AFAB Surgeries

Colloquial Surgery Name: "Top Surgery"

General Description: This is the most common type of surgery among AFAB people. Essentially it serves to flatten the chest and give it a more masculine or neutral appearance. Unlike in a total mastectomy that cisgender women have because of cancer (or another reason), the surgeon often leaves some chest tissue behind and contours it to make it appear more masculine. There are a number of ways the surgery can be performed, which results in a number of different types of scars, recovery timelines, and costs.

Recovery Process: The full recovery for this surgery takes about six weeks, but there is the most soreness and limited movement only for the first three weeks.

Surgery Name: Hysterectomy or Oophorectomy

General Description: This type of surgery removes the uterus and sometimes also the cervix, ovaries, and fallopian tubes, depending on the reason for the procedure. There are many reasons someone might have this procedure, ranging from dysphoria to preventative measures against pregnancy, cervical cancer, and endometriosis. It also can sometimes help increase the masculinizing effects of testosterone by eradicating the primary source of estrogen production.

Recovery Process: A full recovery takes between six and eight weeks, but this is largely dependent on the type of procedure.

Colloquial Surgery Name: "Bottom Surgery"

General Description: This type of surgery is performed in a variety of ways to create a functioning penis. There are a number of very different procedures that prioritize different functions (appearance, sexual pleasure, etc.) and use tissue and skin taken from different parts of the body. There are many options for how this surgery will look and effect someone, so it is best to get information from your VIP's doctor based on what they're looking for.

Recovery Process: Recovery time varies dramatically based on which type of bottom surgery someone receives but will typically range from four to eight weeks.

AMAB Surgeries

Surgery Name: Breast Augmentation

General Description: This type of surgery is perhaps the most familiar. If you've ever heard of a "boob job," you've heard of breast augmentation, and it is relatively common in both transgender and cisgender women. While HRT helps with some breast growth, this procedure helps people have a more feminine-appearing chest.

Recovery Process: Someone who has this surgery will need to rest for two to three days after the procedure and will need to avoid heavy lifting for two weeks.

Surgery Name: Facial Feminization Surgery (FFS)

General Description: FFS is a highly customized set of procedures, often performed in stages rather than all at once, to help change someone's facial structure to appear more typically feminine. Depending on what the person wants, it can include reshaping of the forehead, eyebrows, nose, cheeks, jawline, and Adam's apple.

Recovery Process: Because there are many different procedures that go into FFS, recovery depends on which ones the person chooses. Because the procedures happen in stages, the recovery is also prolonged.

Colloquial Surgery Name: "Bottom Surgery"

General Description: This type of surgery is performed in a variety of ways to create a functioning vagina that can experience sensation. This surgery may happen in stages, and there are a variety of options for types of procedure that depend on someone's target results.

Recovery Process: The full recovery timeline to reach complete functionality is one year, but the first two months are typically the most intense.

HORMONE REPLACEMENT THERAPY

Hormone replacement therapy is a very different process than surgery. While surgery is typically a one-and-done process, HRT is something that many trans folks choose to undergo for the rest of their life. It is not an immediate change, but rather a series of gradual changes over the course of time. Many people—in jest, but also in complete seriousness—refer to starting hormone therapy as "second puberty," which, from personal experience, I can say is painfully accurate. Voice cracks, mood swings, insatiable hunger, and growth spurts (among many other little joys of puberty) were a regular installment in my life for the beginning of my HRT journey.

I was very nervous about starting HRT, and a big part of what scared me was how much of my life I'd spent hearing about how awful testosterone was, how evil it made people, how it was this driver of immaturity and aggression and all manner of negative things. As I talked more to my doctor, I realized that the things I was afraid of fit more closely into the category of "toxic masculinity," and blaming it all on testosterone was giving cis men a free pass to act badly and say, "It's just the testosterone!" when in reality it's connected to how they were socialized, their emotional intelligence, and their impulse control, among other things.

What I have found is that testosterone has turned up the volume on my existing personality and emotions. I sometimes feel anger more strongly if something truly unjust is happening, and when I get protective of my friends I am in *full* protection mode. I describe my journey with T as making me aggressively nice.

While it's different for every person, it's likely that hormone therapy will have some kind of emotional impact, and that sounds scary, but it's important to give your VIP time and space to process the new ways they experience and express emotions. Whether HRT is making it easier or harder to cry or changing the parts of their body where the sensations of different emotions are, it will take some adjusting, and therapy can be an incredible resource to make space for these questions.

When speaking with parents about hormone therapy, I often hear statements like, "Well, my VIP has just been having such a hard time emotionally, and I know that HRT can introduce some new layers of emotions, so we're going to wait for things to even out emotionally before we start HRT." While this is well intentioned, prolonging the wait time can likely exacerbate mental health issues, and many studies have found that going on gender-affirming hormones dramatically improves quality of life and decreases mental health concerns like anxiety or depression.[4] In addition to the many studies on this phenomenon, I can tell you anecdotally for myself and all the trans people in my life that feeling at home in our bodies has incredible positive impacts on our mental health. Beyond just anxiety and depression, gender dysphoria can sometimes manifest as things like OCD, which can then improve when gender dysphoria is alleviated. While these studies and stories are great, it is again important to remember that I do not have access to your VIP's medical history and only their healthcare provider will be able to help you specifically know more about the effects of hormone therapy on their mental health.

If your VIP chooses to go through hormone therapy, it's also important to help them not get too frustrated at the pace of change. As much as I would have loved to wake up with a beard after my first shot, as I'm writing this book, I'm two and a half years in with the beginnings of a patchy goatee. It can be easy to get frustrated as an adult man with the facial hair of a fifteen-year-old boy—until I remind myself that I only started puberty two and a half years ago and I am, in some ways, a fifteen-year-old boy. The changes I want to see are coming, slowly but surely, and I'm in regular conversation with my endocrinologist about how to maximize what I'm looking for. She has been extremely helpful throughout this journey in helping me understand what changes are likely or possible, what changes will require a change in my dosage, and what will require outside factors like changes in diet or exercise. It's important that your VIP has a solid picture of what HRT will and won't do for them.

HRT and Informed Consent

Knowing all the effects and risks of HRT is a key part of the informed consent model of care—a somewhat new framework for determining the right candidates for HRT. Originally, to gain access to HRT, someone needed a formal diagnosis of gender dysphoria from a therapist, which often ended up creating situations where transgender people felt they needed to simplify their identities and avoid asking questions to be allowed access to care. For nonbinary people in particular, there was intense pressure to identify as a binary gender to be allowed access to any sort of gender-affirming care. With the informed consent model, patients instead talk through a full range of questions with their healthcare provider to make sure they understand all the impacts and risks of HRT and then are allowed to give informed consent rather than needing permission from an additional party.

Drawing again from UCSF's resource on transgender care, here are some of the key effects of masculinizing and feminizing hormone therapy through the lenses of physical, emotional, sexual, and reproductive changes.

Feminizing Hormone Therapy (for AMAB people)

Feminizing hormone therapy can consist of a combination of a number of medications, including estrogen, testosterone blockers, and progesterone. Each one impacts the body in a different way, and it's important to talk to your VIP's doctor about which ones make the most sense for them.

- *Likely Physical Changes*: Decreases in skin thickness and oiliness, breast development (eventually, even lactation is possible!), redistribution of weight to hips and thighs, decrease in muscle mass/tone, redistribution of fat in the face to a more feminine shape, and slowing of facial and body hair growth.

• *Likely Emotional Changes*: Vary for the specific person; they may experience a wider range of emotions and different feelings in relationships with other people. Typically instability in personality or mood settles down after the beginning few months of HRT.
• *Likely Sexual Changes*: Potential impacts on where and how pleasure occurs, as well as on sexual orientation or identity.
• *Likely Reproductive Changes*: There is still much that is unknown about the effects of estrogen therapy on fertility, and while some data suggests that sperm counts may be able to return to normal if hormone therapy is stopped, it is best not to assume that this is the case.

Masculinizing Hormone Therapy (for those AFAB)

Because estrogen is not a dominant hormone, the process of introducing a new hormone does not typically require a hormone blocker and most folks go on testosterone specifically. The most common delivery method is an injection, but it is also available in a gel or a patch.

• *Likely Physical Changes*: increased skin thickness and oiliness, temporarily increased acne, weight redistribution away from the hips and thighs, increased facial and body hair growth, some shifts in facial structure, increased muscle mass and strength, voice deepening, potential for hair loss if male pattern baldness is present genetically, changes in sensation of pain or temperature.
• *Likely Emotional Changes*: Sometimes it becomes more challenging to cry or to experience as wide a range of emotions. Typically mood swings or emotional shifts stabilize after the beginning few months of HRT.
• *Likely Sexual Changes*: Increased libido, potential changes in sexual orientation or identity, and different experiences of sexual pleasure.
• *Likely Reproductive Changes*: Slowing and eventual stopping of the menstrual cycle, decreased (but not eliminated) risk of pregnancy. There is limited research available at this time about the impacts of

HRT on fertility, but a growing body of research and real examples indicate that if HRT is stopped it is possible for someone to conceive and deliver a healthy baby.

As with any other medication, there are risks associated with HRT, but many of them are preventable or are specific to genetics, age, and external factors. It is important to speak with your VIP's doctor to get a full picture of their specific risks and what they can do to mitigate them. It's also important to know that rather than a blanket increase of risks across the board, HRT updates your risk profile to be much more like that of the biological sex you're aligning yourself with. For example, I have a higher risk for heart disease than I did before, but it's not abnormally high; it's the normal risk level of a cisgender man. I am also at decreased risk for diseases that typically impact cisgender women.

Despite intentional misinformation to the contrary, hormone therapy is safe and largely reversible, and it has been used for many years. There is a large and ever-growing body of evidence that it is safe and effective in both the short and long terms, and if it is something your VIP wants, it has the potential to *vastly* improve their confidence and quality of life.

STRESS ABOUT MEDICAL TRANSITION

Parents and family members often say to me, "It feels like it's all moving too fast!" in reference to their VIPs asking to talk about surgery or hormone therapy, and I hear what they're saying. It can be a big adjustment, but it's important to remember that just because someone has come out to you recently doesn't mean that they just realized they were trans. In my case, top surgery was something I spent years dreaming of before I brought it up to my parents. It was something I thought about every day, lying in my room crying and looking at pictures online of happy trans men on the beach or at the pool. When I came out to my parents, I initially told them I wasn't interested in any surgeries, and at the time it was true. I was afraid of surgery and not ready for it, but I fairly quickly realized that I was pretty miserable without top surgery.

My parents were not thrilled with me for asking and spent a long time resisting my desire to schedule an initial consultation with a surgeon. From my perspective, they were expressing that I was rushing them; they weren't ready for that conversation and didn't think I was either. To be fully transparent, I love my parents and I love the champion allies they've become, but waiting for top surgery and knowing they were my main barrier in getting it was *extremely* painful for me. Multiple years passed between the first time I asked them about top surgery and my first consultation with my surgeon—If I'd had to wait much longer, I am not sure our relationship would have been able to survive that.

Your VIP has likely been thinking or learning about the care they're requesting long before bringing it up to you, and if you have specific concerns that are preventing you from supporting them on this part of their journey, it is best to reach out to a qualified medical specialist who can talk through your concerns and calm your worries.

MEDICAL PROCEDURE REGRET

I want to briefly touch on regret about gender-affirming medical procedures because there is a significant amount of misinformation about how frequently people regret their medical transition. According to the Associated Press, a review of twenty-seven studies involving eight thousand transgender people who had surgeries, 1 percent, on average, expressed regret. For some of the individuals in that group, the regret was temporary, while an even smaller group went on to seek reversal surgeries.[5]

Though the attention being drawn to those who detransition makes it seem like a common phenomenon, the reality is that this is availability bias in action—the more we hear about it, the more we think it happens—and this is an infrequent phenomenon. A 2021 study by Fenway Health found that while around 13 percent of transgender people have at some point detransitioned, 85 percent of those respondents reported detransitioning because of familial pressure, safety concerns, or a lack of support. As the researchers put it, "These findings show that detransition and transition regret are not synonymous, despite the two phenomena being frequently conflated in the media and in political debates."[6] In short, it is extremely uncommon for someone to regret their transition, and this is not a good reason to avoid supporting your VIP.

Not every person is going to want to have every surgery, but for those that do want certain procedures, the evidence continues to mount that these procedures bring massive improvements in mental health and quality of life—including 73 percent lower risk of suicidality.[7] It is crucial to remember that gender-affirming care is safe, gender-affirming care is well researched, and gender-affirming care saves lives.

ALTERNATIVE METHODS OF DYSPHORIA REDUCTION

In addition to medical procedures, there are other ways your VIP might be able to approximate the physical results they're looking for.

- If they're hoping for more facial hair, mascara can be very effective at darkening the hair that may already be present or at creating a natural "shadow." If they're hoping for less facial hair, laser hair removal is a longer-term (though more painful) alternative to shaving.
- If they're hoping to reduce the size of their chest, they can try Trans-Tape or a chest binder, which is a compression tank top. It is important that your VIP follows the guidelines for safe use: Do not sleep in them, never machine dry them (I made that error), try to limit use to eight to twelve hours a day, and take rest days whenever possible.
- If they're hoping to minimize the size of their genitalia, they can try tucking underwear, which helpfully secure the genitals in a way that makes them not show up in clothing or bathing suits.
- If they're hoping to simulate the appearance of breasts, there are a number of ways to pad a bra to create a natural look.
- If they're hoping for a deeper or higher voice, voice therapy is an excellent way to harness strategies like breath management to achieve the desired sound.

Before we close out this chapter, I'd be remiss if I didn't share another Joy Exercise. While so much of the conversation we have nationally around medical care is high stress and high intensity, often discussing how miserable people are without access to it, there is so much more to the story. With access to proper gender-affirming care, I feel like I have come home to my body and truly recognize myself for the first time. That is really magical, and something I want to make sure we take time to celebrate.

JOY EXERCISES: COMING HOME TO OUR BODIES

For those who want it, transition-related gender-affirming care can be absolutely magical. Looking in the mirror and recognizing myself for the first time, learning to shave my new beard, and going swimming without a shirt on were huge milestones that I was so excited to celebrate with the people I love. Here are a few quick suggestions for ways you can celebrate these moments:

1. If your VIP has started testosterone, give them a shaving kit or carve out special time to teach them how to shave.
2. Remind your VIP to take progress pictures and videos throughout the process of hormone replacement therapy. Changes can feel very slow, and your VIP may not notice them at first; looking back at old pictures and videos is a great way to see just how far they've come.
3. Help coordinate a photo shoot for your VIP to celebrate looking and feeling more authentic to how they identify. Consider replacing old family photos with new ones taken together where they feel more seen.
4. If your VIP is musically inclined, changes in voice can sometimes be stressful. Have a mini concert where you celebrate the new songs they're able to sing with their vocal range.

9

FINDING JOY

Throughout this book, I've shared a handful of "joy exercises" to help ground us in joy, but I want to spend some time here talking about why that matters. Throughout the long, troubled history of humanity, there have been powerful stories of resistance—notably, resistance that takes the shape of a group of people doing something they are specifically forced not to do.

Rosa Parks staying at the front of the bus, Jews praying when it was forbidden, people refusing to fight when drafted for war—resistance is defined, in part, by a refusal to accept an oppressive rule or reality. For the LGBTQ+ community, they've come for so many parts of our lives: our ability to gather safely at gay bars and queer spaces, our ability to perform and enjoy drag shows, our ability to get married or adopt children, and, for transgender people, our ability to access life-changing and life-saving medical care to help us find home in our bodies. There is an all-out war targeting everything that brings our community joy in the hope of making us feel so beaten down, hopeless, and joyless that we just quit fighting back. This means that laughing, dancing, celebrating, and being joyful are direct acts of resistance.

When we talk about ways to celebrate and have fun even in the face of challenging situations, these aren't just coping strategies to get through those moments and protect our mental health—they're ways to take back our power and refuse to let them win and take our joy. Trans joy can fall into a number of "buckets," so to speak, and I'll share those here as well as some specific ways to find joy in each of those buckets.

1. I love myself as I am, and I am worthy of that love.
2. Others love me as I am, and I am worthy of that love.
3. I am not the only one like myself.
4. I get to have dreams about my future that can come true.
5. I can experience ease and pleasure in my life.
6. I am taken care of, and I can take care of others.
7. I can give love to my inner child.

My goal in this chapter is not to write a recipe book of all the possible configurations of trans joy but rather to share with you the skills for cooking so you can write your own recipes. For each category, I'll share what it means and why it matters, as well as a few starter suggestions, but it'll be up to you and your VIP to figure out how to create each of the feelings above for them specifically.

I LOVE MYSELF AS I AM.

I love myself. What a loaded, powerful statement. There is so much here that's beyond your control as an external force, and increasing self-esteem in young people is a topic that countless people have made entire careers out of and still haven't found the perfect answer. We're not going to solve that problem here, but we can certainly start to be a part of the solution.

For trans folks, self-esteem can be a bit of a minefield. Our bodies can be major sources of dysphoria, our personalities often differ from the norm and can be sources for bullying or harassment, even our basic humanity is often up for debate.

In terms of our physical confidence, medical transition (or lack thereof) can obviously be a make-or-break for some trans folks. For me, I knew I was not really going to be able to feel confident until I had my top surgery, because I so strongly hated the way I looked and the way clothes fit my body. Some of that was unavoidable, but there were ways I could style clothes to emphasize or deemphasize the parts of my body I liked more or less. Gender-affirming clothing and haircuts are hugely crucial for folks building (and maintaining) their confidence.

Joy Exercises

Take a trip to the mall or to a clothing swap and help your VIP find clothing options that make them feel confident.

Find a combination of cisgender and transgender people with a similar body structure as your VIP who can act as a "style icon" and help your VIP learn what styles of clothing work with their body type. It can be a celebrity, someone on social media, or someone you know in real life!

There is also so much more to self-love than just loving our bodies, and there is so much more to us than just the bodies that carry us through the world. Our personalities, or passions, our creativity and our brilliance—there are infinite things to love about ourselves if we know where to look.

Joy Exercise

Develop a shared practice of morning affirmations or picking five things you and your VIP like about yourselves today, to remind your VIP that things are not *all* bad and help pull them out of loops of self-criticism.

If you notice specific things your VIP loves about themselves, like their artistic ability or their problem-solving skills, try to create situations, both explicitly and subtly, where they get to lean into those talents.

OTHERS LOVE ME AS I AM.

This may be perhaps the broadest of all the categories, because being loved by others encapsulates so many layers and so many "steps" that come before it. Before someone can love you as they are, they need to *see* you as you are. For your VIP, that might look like consistently correct name and pronoun usage or something similar. For me, I am joyous when I am regularly called "Sir" or other masculine terms by strangers.

Once someone truly sees you as you are, then they have the ability to love the true you. This means not just a begrudging acceptance or loving someone in spite of their identity, but loving them *because of it*. There are lots of ways this might show up, and there are so many different types of love. Romantically, many people want to know they are worthy of being loved and that it is possible to have someone fall in love with them. For a long time, I accepted subpar treatment from people who loved me in spite of my trans identity, largely because I had never seen an example of a trans person being loved in a beautiful and authentic way in real life or in any of the media I was consuming.

When I eventually fell in love with someone who loved all of me for who I was, it was revolutionary. Realizing that I deserved and was capable of love in the same way my cisgender peers were—which sounds like it should be obvious but wasn't—was incredible.

Joy Exercise

Find positive, age-appropriate media representation of trans people in loving, healthy relationships.

There are so many other types of love besides romantic love, and at least one of those types of love is likely what drew you to purchase this book. Platonic and familial love are just as powerful and just as important in making a person feel loved from every angle. Find opportunities to reflect both privately and together with your VIP about the things their journey has added to your life.

Joy Exercise

Mark the date when your VIP came out (or another notable date in their journey) and celebrate the anniversary. This sends a clear message that you view their coming out as a good thing worth remembering and celebrating.

I AM NOT THE ONLY ONE LIKE MYSELF.

Positive representation can make a whole world of difference for someone. Seeing someone else just like us be loved, be funny, be cool, go on adventures, and do whatever else we aspire to helps us realize and remember that it's possible for us too. As we spoke about in earlier chapters, community is an extremely powerful armor against loneliness and hopelessness, and there are so many reasons why. Seeing people who are actively going through the same things as us means we have people who we don't need to explain things to and people who can give us advice or insights from their own journeys. It also shows us that if someone else has and is surviving through what we're going through, we can do it too.

Joy Exercises

Start a family tradition of a movie night or book club where members of your family can take turns choosing a piece of media that makes them feel seen and enjoy it together.

Help your VIP find fun and creative ways to tell and share their own story or stories that make them feel seen, whether it's through writing, making videos, or another format.

I GET TO HAVE DREAMS ABOUT MY FUTURE THAT CAN COME TRUE.

Growing up as a young trans kid, even though I was fortunate enough to have support in my current moment, I didn't have the language to even begin to dream about my future. I had a giant blank spot where my career, wedding, family, travels, and appearance were supposed to be. Because I had seen literally no examples of trans people growing up beyond the age of twenty-two, especially trans men, I didn't bother dreaming about my own future. It simply didn't feel real.

Then I saw an off-Broadway play that featured a transgender man playing a trans character who had a happy ending, and my mind was blown. I was so excited, and I spent the whole show sitting in my seat planning out everything I was going to say to him after the show. I was going to say, "I've never seen myself represented on a stage before. It gives me so much hope for myself, and for my future as a transgender man. Thank you." When he came out from backstage after the show, I was all ready to give him my spiel. I took one look at him, opened my mouth, and just started sobbing. I couldn't get a word out, but he saw me and came right up to me and started crying too. He pulled me in, and we just stood there crying in each other's arms, not saying a word but understanding everything we needed to know about each other. After a few minutes, he stepped back and said, "This is it. This is why representation matters." And he told me the story of how the exact same thing happened to him the first time he saw a transgender person on stage, twenty years before, and the difference that made for him.

That moment opened so much for me in how I could imagine myself growing up, growing old, finding love, succeeding, finding joy. That moment is largely what inspired me to become the speaker and advocate I am today and helped me dream a future for myself as a public speaker who gets to be that moment for as many young trans people as possible.

Joy Exercise

Find ways for your VIP to learn about, see, or meet older members of the LGBTQ+ community who share their identity or interests to show them positive possibility models.

I CAN EXPERIENCE EASE AND PLEASURE IN MY LIFE.

This is perhaps the simplest of the categories. Because of all the hate we get, all the teaching we have to do, and all the things we need to be hypervigilant about for the sake of our own safety, it is an unexpected treat when things are *easy*. The underlying sentiment behind this type of joy is just having the reminder that not everything is going to be a fight and that the fights we are in now will not go on forever. It will not always be this hard to access healthcare, or to pick out clothes at the store, or to find somewhere to work or live. We'll continue to explore ways you can set up these supportive structures in different parts of your VIP's life and ways you can get involved in building a better world long term, but there are also small steps you can take toward finding this feeling today.

Joy Exercises

- Seek out services from queer-affirming or queer-owned businesses where you know your VIP will be seen and respected. This will hopefully take at least some of the hypervigilance off their plate.
- If you have a really positive interaction with someone while speaking about your VIP, or hear someone say something nice about them, make sure to let them know so they have as much evidence as possible that there are so many supportive people in the world around them.

I AM TAKEN CARE OF, AND I CAN TAKE CARE OF OTHERS.

This one encapsulates a lot of things. Again, feeling safe is a key part of the foundation of this category of joy, as it can be hard to feel truly taken care of when there are things that make us feel unsafe. Some of the other categories we discussed talk about the power of community, but largely through the lens of visibility or receiving support. While those things are wonderful, there is also so much more to community than that. This type of joy comes from being actively involved in the love that flows through a community, on both the giving and receiving ends. It's crucial to find a balance here: No one wants to feel like a burden, nor do they want to feel like they spend all their time taking care of others. This doesn't mean you need to quantify how much care you're doing and make sure you're hitting net neutral at the end of the month, nor does it mean you need to make sure that the type of care you receive is the same as the type of care you give. It simply means knowing that where possible, you can ask for what you need and know that others can ask you for support in return.

Joy Exercise

Start a regular gratitude practice with your VIP to help you both realize the extent of the care you receive and all its different forms. Whether it's journaling or writing thank-you notes or texts, spend time feeling grateful.

I love to cook for people. One of my favorite ways to take care of people is to feed them good food that's perfectly aligned to their palates. Cooking for a huge dinner party or to make portions and drop them off at friends' houses can be a grounding ritual for me that helps me decompress after a long day or big event. I don't need these friends to cook for me in return (and between you and me, I don't really *want* some of them to cook for me, if you catch my drift). The type of care I often need is time where I can turn my brain off—quality time where I can forget about everything bothering me or scaring me or making me angry and just play a board game or lose at Mario Kart.

Joy Exercise

Make a regular habit of taking care of your community with your VIP. Whether it's by participating in mutual aid groups, volunteering to help organize clothes at a community closet, or something else, practice taking care of the people who take care of you.

I CAN GIVE LOVE TO MY INNER CHILD.

This is an interesting one, and there's so much more to it than what I have the space or expertise for, but there is a knowledge among queer people that aging and time work a little differently for us, for a variety of reasons. Many formative young-person-experiences are not ones that we have access to. Whether it's because we were consciously excluded, were too uncomfortable or dysphoric to join, or were told we have to grow up and be very mature to advocate for ourselves, we feel the impact of losing "normal" childhood experiences in many unique ways.

I'll walk you through a couple stories of how this shows up for me and has throughout my life. On a factual level, I didn't grow up as a little boy. My parents didn't have an extremely gendered parenting style, and it's not like I couldn't have access to "little boy" things if I asked for them at home, but at school the teachers and other students all followed a preexisting social order that I fit myself into. Part of the order I fit into involved things I liked (playing with Webkinz at recess was a delight until I hit fourth grade) and other things I resisted (princess dress-up parties, makeup, talking about boys), but each thing I resisted or that fell outside of the order was an exception, not the rule. For trans women, this type of exclusion often shows up as having missed out on the formative and quintessential experience of a girls' slumber party.

Joy Exercise

Talk to your VIP about whether there are things they feel like they missed out on in childhood (or are currently missing out on, depending on their age). Whether it's a slumber party, a Nerf gun fight, or learning how to start a fire, make it a point to do these things together or to help organize the activity for your VIP and their trusted friends.

In my teenage years, after I came out, I continued to miss out on things. Dating as an LGBTQ+ person in a small town meant the pool was extremely limited, and I received no education on what a healthy relationship looked like, so in college, I made dating choices that more closely resembled those of an irresponsible teenager because I hadn't had the chance to be an irresponsible teenager and learn the lessons that come along with those mistakes.

I also avoided anything that might resemble youthful rebellion because I was focused on being as acceptable as possible. My job was to become perfectly patient and a perfect educator, which meant that I entered my adult life with very few boundaries. As I say in therapy, I was a bit of a doormat.

Joy Exercise

Find a way that feels authentic to you and your VIP to honor their inner child. One idea is to have a whole bunch of surprise "birthday parties" for each year before they transitioned, with each one having a different, affirming theme.

Another unexpected way this shows up is through learning household tasks. The division of household labor is often very gendered, and many trans folks get to adulthood not knowing anything about cooking, or cleaning, or home repair. Though I'm an advocate for everyone being well-rounded and competent rather than encouraging you to just teach them "their new role," it can still be joyful to make specific time to teach them skills they might have previously missed out on that they're excited about.

Hopefully this list has given you enough tools to talk to your VIP and help them find all the joy they're looking for. Use these tips as starter ideas to help you develop your own joy practices, and your VIP will guide you to find things that bring you joy together. Remember too that joy exercises must fit into a larger allyship strategy to make a meaningful impact; both are pieces of an overall strategy to make sure your VIP feels seen, supported, and loved exactly as they are.

SUPPORTING
TRANS YOUTH
IN THE WORLD

What to Expect and What You Can Do

10

LIVING AS A TRANSGENDER PERSON AND UNDERSTANDING CURRENT STIGMA

Content warning: Parts of this chapter may be challenging to read. Transphobia in the United States is hitting an all-time high, and looking at the number of hateful bills proposed and the increase in anti-trans violence is upsetting. As a trans person who used to live in a very liberal state, I tried to keep my head in the sand for as long as possible, and while that kept me comfortable, it did not keep me safe. That mentality meant I avoided addressing transphobia where I saw it in my city and that everyone turned a blind eye to the hateful bills proposed in the South and Midwest until they had spread too far to ignore. As we talk through the ways hate and misinformation are spread, you may feel tempted to look away, and while it is crucial to listen to yourself and know when you're at your capacity, it is also crucial for the sake of your VIP that you understand the full picture of what's going on.

At the time of writing this chapter in the spring of 2023, we're in the midst of one of the most intense waves of anti-trans sentiment ever seen in this country. With every bit of optimism left in my heart, I hope these bills are nothing but an unfortunate memory by the time you're reading this. With every bit of realism in my heart, I know that's unlikely. Knowing how frequently the political landscape can shift, rather than dwelling on the specifics of select bills that may or may not still be relevant by the time you're reading this, I'm instead going to focus in general about how we got to where we are, the tools of misinformation driving the anti-trans movement, and how (and when) to respond to points of general transphobia as they come up.

This approach aligns with my general approach to speaking about anti-transgender legislation, because the people writing and pushing this legislation should never be taken at face value. They have one goal, and it's not protecting kids, or protecting women, or athletic fairness, or preventing sexual assault, or any of the other noble taglines they attach to their hateful campaigns. Speaking at the 2023 Conservative Political Action Conference, Michael Knowles finally spoke his truth when he said, "For the good of society . . . transgenderism must be eradicated from public life entirely—the whole preposterous ideology, at every level." This statement was met with riotous applause.[1] All these bills, all their misinformation, is solely aimed at building public support for the complete erasure of the transgender community and the broader LGBTQ+ community.

CRUELLA DE VIL

When I speak with people about any of the hundreds of pieces of anti-trans legislation, I don't respond to or debate the content of these bills and instead focus on the broader implications and messaging. To explain how and why, I want to walk through a quick analogy about a classic movie villain: Cruella de Vil. (For the less Disney-inclined among us, Cruella de Vil is known for hating dogs, and specifically for wanting to have a coat made from dalmatian fur.)

Cruella's goal, in this analogy, has always been to get rid of dalmatians, but everybody loves dalmatians, and if she started out by publicly stating that we needed to get rid of all the dalmatians, everyone would rally against that blatant act of hate and violence.

Instead of outright calling for the elimination of dalmatians, she starts a rumor that thousands of dalmatians have been driving cars and getting into accidents. She shares her suspicions that many of them are driving while under the influence and that they're dangerous. She proposes legislation to ban dalmatians from driving cars because of how often they get DUIs. The politicians who support dalmatians debate her on her points, sharing statistics about how few dalmatian DUIs there've been and how many dalmatians are safe drivers. Largely missing from this debate is information about how the notion of a dalmatian driving a car is preposterous and essentially isn't occurring at all.

The debates are publicized on social media, television, and newspapers, and the general public hears all about the "dalmatian debate." They assume that because it is called a debate, there are two sides talking about how to solve a problem—in this case, the problem of dalmatian DUIs. Many of them become scared or angry—they don't want a dalmatian driving through *their* neighborhood. Cruella tells people that their children are at risk because dalmatians love to drive through school zones, and using that fear, she builds support to take away the driver's licenses of dalmatians. With this support, she starts to ask the next question: Why do so many dalmatians drive under the influence? Why do they want to drive through school zones? Perhaps they shouldn't be allowed in school zones at all, or even on the roads. They're dangerous.

Again, her opposition debates her on the merits of her points, and despite how many contrary facts there are—that almost zero dalmatians have DUIs, that very few dalmatians drive at all, that most of them just want to be allowed to live their lives and have no desire to hurt children—the debate is again publicized. People assume the two sides are fighting from equal factual grounds, and given how much they've already heard about the awful dalmatians getting DUIs in school zones, they're even more angry and scared of the dalmatians. They support Cruella's bills.

When Cruella announces that dalmatians are a danger to society and should be removed, she already has much of the general public behind her—not because of any number of facts or logic, but because of a perfectly executed misinformation campaign. The "debate" was normalized every step of the way, people assumed she was solving a problem that existed, and they believed her when she said we needed to get rid of the dalmatians. Her goal from the beginning was to eliminate dalmatians from public life, and she achieved that.

What we've seen over the past few years with anti-trans legislation is the same thing: "debating" problems that *do not exist* to build hate and anger toward the transgender community, a strategy that has since been openly admitted by the leaders of the anti-trans movement. If you'd like to look through the evidence of this, news outlet Mother Jones published a leak of thousands of emails from some of the major players in the space of anti-trans advocacy, including the American College of Pediatrics, the Heritage Foundation, and the Alliance Defending Freedom.[2] I would encourage you to look at that article and research the other groups listed here if you are interested in learning more about this small group of real-life Cruella de Vils. We spent years debating transgender sports bills on their actual merits, but they were only ever about putting a foot in the door to create an image of a violent group of people stealing trophies, threatening children, and deceiving everyone for their own personal gain.

If you need evidence that this was their strategy, look no further than simple numbers. There have been zero instances of people pretending to be transgender just to win a trophy, and not a single legislator who proposed a sports ban could name an example of a transgender K–12 athlete dominating the competition in their own state or any other. In fact, in most states that proposed legislation to ban transgender athletes from K–12 athletics, there are countably few transgender athletes playing sports at all, fewer than half of whom were in women's sports. In Missouri, for example, there were five athletes who applied to be able to switch to playing sports with peers of the same gender identity. Can you imagine any other type of legislation being introduced specifically to target *literally five children*?

The people proposing and supporting these bills are well aware of the fact that they are solving a problem that doesn't exist, yet when they speak about these bills, they paint a dramatic portrait of a nation filled with disingenuous transgender athletes coming to make sure that *your daughter* misses out on a college scholarship. They know they are solving a problem that doesn't exist, but they spent years building a foundation of fear and anger toward a community that threatens sports, fairness, and other children in this way and have built a base that supports—or at least is open to—far more hateful legislation.

This type of public debate and normalization of the idea that there are two sides to these issues is one of the strongest moves in the larger playbook of strategies for erasing transgender and LGBTQ+ people from public life completely. Fighting against this playbook could easily be a whole book on its own, so I'm not going to dive too deep here; for the remainder of this chapter I'm going to discuss the element of the playbook that is likely to show up the most in your day-to-day allyship if it hasn't already: misinformation.

There are a variety of ways misinformation can (and will) show up, but I want to begin with some definitions to make sure we're on the same page about what we're up against.

Misinformation: Information that is unintentionally or unknowingly false
Disinformation: False information deliberately spread to deceive or mislead people

Simply put, spreading misinformation is being wrong but not knowing it, while spreading disinformation is intentionally lying to build fear, anger, or support for an issue. While we may use these words interchangeably in conversation, they are very different in their intent and in the strategies we must use to address them.

Most of the folks we're going to talk about in this chapter—and the ones you're most likely to be able to get through to—are those in misinformed category. They aren't necessarily hateful people and are hopefully open to learning correct information. The folks in the disinformation category are far more likely—if not guaranteed—to have nefarious motives and be much harder to get through to with correct information because they are not seeking to meet you on the battleground of facts.

HOW TO IDENTIFY PEOPLE WHO ARE OPEN TO LEARNING FROM YOU

Later in this chapter, we're going to discuss some conversational strategies and questions for getting through to people who may have been on the receiving end of lots of misinformation, but I want to highlight that these are strategies that work best under the right conditions. They work only if the person you're speaking to is genuinely open to learning or, at a bare minimum, curious. Rarely do people go into conversations ready to have their minds changed, but these people are more likely to be open to at least hearing your perspective, especially if they feel you're open to theirs.

Sometimes, people debate in bad faith, which essentially means having absolutely no intention of reaching an agreement. Some people see a debate as entertainment, others are just looking to get a reaction from you, and still others will use sneaky logical fallacies to confuse you and make it seem like they won. As an example, conservative commentator Ben Shapiro loves to invite people to "debate" him, with a goal of generating shareable content for his social media, making his opponent embarrassingly flustered by saying things that are a whole new level of absurd, and "owning the libs" with a dramatic logical fallacy.

Thankfully, not everyone is as nefarious as Shapiro, but that also means it isn't always as easy to tell whether someone is talking to you in good faith or not. There are a few indicators you may be able to use, and while these aren't going to be 100 percent accurate, they're a good place to start.

- How does the person you're speaking to respond to your points or questions? If they're smirking, scoffing, or laughing when you speak, that may indicate they aren't taking you seriously and showing up with respect for what you have to say.
- Are they willing to speak to you in private? Generally, folks who are "trolling," or purposely trying to annoy you, want an audience for the show they're trying to get you to put on. If they're willing to talk one-on-one, that may indicate that their priority is speaking with you and having this conversation.
- What physical signifiers do they have? People who have displays like satirical pronouns in their social media profiles or wearing clothing with inflammatory statements are hoping to get attention or a reaction and are likely not interested in having a genuine conversation.
- Are they making violent statements? Your safety needs to be the priority, and unfortunately some people have been radicalized to a point where they may want to harm people they view as "pushing an agenda." Pay close attention to violent words in the language they're using and excuse yourself if necessary.

As a friendly reminder, while there are plenty of people out in the real world who I do believe are open to having conversations and changing their beliefs, those people are rarely—if ever—going to be found in internet comments sections. Social media comments are full of rage-baiters who want to make you mad because it's *fun* for them. No matter how good it feels in the moment to "clap back," it's just going to leave you feeling drained. I promise, it's not worth it. Log off.

HOW TO GET THROUGH TO THEM

When I have conversations to combat misinformation, my priority is asking questions. Sometimes in life, a "work backward" approach can be helpful when you know where you want to be and have to figure out how to get there, but working backward in these conversations implies that you know exactly where you're starting. While it might be easy to assume that everyone is just being confused, hateful, or bigoted for the same reasons, there are often a wide variety of factors that lead to someone believing misinformation, few of them truly hateful.

I ask a few types of questions when I speak with people about misinformation to figure out what might be driving this for them.

Information-Gathering Questions

I want to understand where the person is coming from, and the person that I'm talking to wants to feel heard, so I ask questions and genuinely listen to the answers. This is also how I begin to understand some of their underlying fears or beliefs. Questions might include:

- Why do you say that?
- I don't think I've heard that statistic before; could you tell me more about where you heard that?
- What do you think is the worst-case scenario here?
- Where do you think that concern is coming from?
- How would you feel if it was your own child?

Media Literacy Questions

Because I went to primary school post-Google, a key part of our curriculum was media literacy—identifying high-quality sources, potential author biases, and fake news. Unfortunately, not everyone has had access to that type of education, and even fewer have chosen to continue using those skills. With these types of questions, I model some of the questions I ask myself when assessing a new source, such as:

- What questions does this article leave you with? Is there anything that feels hard to believe?
- What are the credentials of the experts cited in this article?
- How many participants were in this research study? Was it peer reviewed by a reputable journal?
- Are there other studies or articles that have found similar things, or do they contradict each other?

Misinformation-Specific Questions

Once I've determined that someone is open to learning and has been engaging with the questions I ask them in good faith, I ask questions more specifically to help debunk the misinformation I've learned they're exposed to by using the underlying fears or misconceptions they've shared with me.

- If they assume that because they hear a lot about a problem it is very widespread, I ask something like, "How many trans athletes do you believe there are at the K–12 level in your state? How about in the country?"
- If they're upset by the GOP horror stories of frequent genital surgeries on young children, I could ask, "How many kids do you believe have had gender-affirming surgeries and at what ages? What types of surgeries are there?"
- If their primary concern is about fairness and safety for female athletes, I might ask, "I agree that we should keep women and girls safe! Do forced genital exams sound like protecting women and girls in sports? Do you put similar amounts of energy into advocating for equal funding and pay for women's sports teams?"

There isn't space here to talk through every potential underlying belief someone might have that would lead them to believe misinformation or support anti-trans policies, but I would love to walk through a longer example to show how someone with good intentions might be radicalized by misinformation.

For this example, I'll point to a frantic email I received from a parent after I delivered a speech. She let me know that she had truly loved the speech and wanted to be supportive, but she had recently heard about an initiative driven by the transgender community to make schools in Australia eliminate the words "Mom" and "Dad" from school vocabulary. She was terrified that supporting the trans inclusion movement would mean losing her ability to be a mom, something that was crucial to her identity.

I knew her intentions were good and suspected misinformation was afoot, so I did some research of my own to figure out where these fears were coming from. The original proposal encouraged Australian teachers to say, "your parents" or "your grown-ups" when speaking broadly to students instead of "your mom and dad," as a movement to include:

- Children living in foster homes
- Children of LGBTQ+ couples
- Children with single parents
- Children being raised by aunts, uncles, siblings, or grandparents

That small change in language, which doesn't have any impact on what kids call their own parents, seems like a no-brainer in terms of the impact it would have on making all students feel seen and not "othered" in school. The anti-trans crowd knows it may be hard to use this simple proposal to create any momentum for their movement, but with a little tweaking, it just might. Enter a cluster of news articles called "cancel culture comes for mum and dad," focusing on "how absurd it is that you can no longer call your own mum 'mum.'"[3] These articles, in turn, go viral worldwide as an example of yet another thing that the trans community wants to "cancel," and when the audience for these articles is people who have no exposure to the trans community, the result is a global population of people who might otherwise be allies but have fallen victim to intentional misinformation and are now quite afraid of transgender people taking away important parts of their identity.

After developing an understanding of where this woman's fear was coming from, I shared with her some articles about the *actual* proposal and explained how intentional this misinformation was—all without judging her or accusing her of anything. She hadn't sought out that misinformation, but it was everywhere and she couldn't avoid it. We talked through her fears, and after a twenty-minute Zoom call she was proud to call herself an ally.

I easily could have chosen to call her statement transphobic, challenge her for the beliefs she brought into the conversation, or judge her for falling prey to what felt (to me) like obvious misinformation, but that would likely have made her feel lots of shame and ended our conversation immediately. It may even have made her dig her heels in and pushed her further away from showing up as an ally. By choosing to make her feel safe to ask questions without fear of judgment, I could help her become the well-informed ally she knew she wanted to be.

Remember, misinformation does not spread by accident or by inherent moral failing. Billions of dollars and entire companies are devoted solely to researching, developing, and spreading the most effective kinds of misinformation. It makes sense that they would be good at their jobs. They know exactly how to tap into the fears or misconceptions people may already hold and lead them to a desired endpoint.

DEBUNKING AND PRE-BUNKING

Misinformation is like a virus in how it spreads and behaves—its spread can be rapid and explosive, and it evolves over time to spread in the most effective way possible. As an example of the evolution of the anti-trans movement, a few conservative personalities on Twitter began saying, "OK, Groomer" as a joking rage-bait to LGBTQ+ activists, but when it caught on with their followers, they immediately shifted their language and debate strategies to prominently feature descriptions of LGBTQ+ people, their families, and their allies as "groomers." Now this language regularly comes up in serious political settings, and many people truly believe that LGBTQ+ people are groomers. The virus mutated to spread as effectively as possible.

The good news about the metaphor of misinformation as a virus means that there's another parallel: vaccines! Just like vaccines have a known protective effect against viruses, there are ways we can protect ourselves and others from misinformation before it strikes.

You've likely heard the word "debunking" before, which refers to the act of proving a myth or misconception wrong, but it is often an uphill battle to correct something once people have learned the wrong information. Recently, there's been an increase in our conversation about "pre-bunking"— giving people access to the correct information *first*, which makes them significantly less likely to believe misinformation when they read it.

This means that having proactive conversations with the people you work with, your family members, your friends, your fellow congregation-members—really, anyone who will listen—is crucial to stopping the spread of misinformation. Find ways that feel authentic to you to spread accurate information, whether it's by sharing informative articles on social media (and offering to answer questions for those who are curious), by sharing your story in a public speaking capacity, or something else entirely.

According to Laura Garcia, writing on the website First Draft,

> A good prebunk addresses people's concerns, speaks to their lived experience and compels them to share that knowledge. Prebunks are empowering: The whole point is about building trust with your audience instead of simply correcting facts.
>
> There are three main types of prebunks:
>
> 1. Fact-based: correcting a specific false claim or narrative
> 2. Logic-based: explaining tactics used to manipulate
> 3. Source-based: pointing out bad sources of information[4]

As you're having conversations with people in your life—both those who are actively unsupportive and those who aren't entirely sure what's going on—pre-bunking by sharing accurate information and explicitly warning them about new deception techniques they're likely to see can be extremely helpful.

WORKING THROUGH FEELINGS OF HOPELESSNESS

I'm not sure how things are in the world you're sitting in—and hopefully if I do my job well, things are at least *slightly* improved—but in my world today things are looking rough. As I am writing this chapter, my home state of

Missouri has just passed two terrible bills—one that bans access to healthcare for transgender youth and one that bans transgender athletes in grades K–12 from participating in sports. It is exhausting to travel to our state capitol week after week and hear my legislators say things I would not dare repeat in the pages of this book (or, quite frankly, ever), wondering when the bill will come that drives me out of the state searching for safety.

I've been going through a wide range of emotions over the past couple of years. I've been scared, sad, angry, vengeful, desperate, exhausted, and completely numb. I've felt a lot of things, sometimes all at once, but one of the things I've never been is hopeless.

While social media and the news may make it so easy to fall into gloom and despair, it's important to remember that making you upset keeps you engaged. You are more likely to stay on social media after seeing a terrifying tweet, you're more likely to watch a whole TikTok or YouTube video if it contains upsetting content, and one 2023 study found that every negative word in a headline increased the clickthrough rate by 2.3 percent, which is *huge* in marketing terms.[5] There is good news out there, and there is news out there that isn't as bad as it is made out to be, but that doesn't sell papers or get likes, so it's less likely to be reported.

Don't get me wrong: I'm not saying things are peachy—all systems are indeed red, all hands are needed on deck—but this fight is so far from a done deal, and we are seeing victories every day. Throughout history, there has been a target on the back of the LGBTQ+ community. Sometimes the target is bigger or more visible, sometimes it focuses on a specific part of the community, but we have fought these battles before, and we have always won in the end. There has never been a question in my mind that we will win this war; the question for me has instead been what it will cost us: the time we'll sacrifice, the joy we'll miss, the people we'll lose.

The biggest source of hope for me in this movement has been taking care of others, finding my community, and reminding myself every day that this was never meant to be a problem that one person could solve. Being involved in political organizing in my state has been challenging in many ways, but seeing the number of passionate and brilliant minds fighting with and for my community, arm in arm, has made me feel so secure in our inevitable victory. I also trust them enough to know that when I take a break or a vacation it doesn't mean all progress will come to a halt. We carry the torch together.

No matter how hard they try to take away your hope, to make you feel alone—and believe me *they are trying*—know that all hope is never lost and that there are millions of people in every corner of this country and of this world who are fighting tooth and nail to build a world where you and your VIP know you belong. Hold onto that hope as long as you can.

11

GOING TO SCHOOL AS A TRANSGENDER PERSON

School is foundational place for young people. For many, it's a place of learning, exploring new passions and subject areas, finding social connections, and exploring concepts of identity. For many LGBTQ+ students, however, it can be a major source of stress. It can be home to judgment, gossip, or bullying from students and faculty alike, and many transgender students face uphill battles to have their names, pronouns, and identities affirmed.

In this chapter, we'll talk through a number of best practices for supporting your VIP in the school environment, as well as when and how to call on your allies for support. As we walk through the challenges you might face, it's important to remember that even if you don't win every battle, showing up and trying every time nonetheless sends a clear message to your VIP that they are worth fighting for and helps them get through the challenging years of school. The act of having people, or even just one person, on their side can make a massive difference in their mental health and resilience.

The process of coming out at school—or of not being able to come out at school—can be challenging and anxiety inducing for many young people. Here are a few reminders to share with your VIP:

1. Your identity or experience are no more or less real because you are or aren't out of the closet. If you come out, it should be because you want to.
2. It's okay if you don't know exactly what label you want to use yet, or if that label changes at any time. Being a kid and a teenager are perfect times to explore your identity and figure out what feels right for you, and everyone around you is doing this in their own way. Don't be afraid to try new hobbies, styles, or making new friends!

HOW GENDER SHOWS UP AT SCHOOL

In addition to learning math, science, and reading skills, children come to school to learn social rules and norms, how to form meaningful relationships, and hundreds of other little lessons they pick up from the words, actions, and structures present around them. These lessons are known as the "hidden curriculum": the unwritten, unofficial, and often unintended norms, values, and beliefs that students are taught in school.

Gender is perhaps one of the biggest elements of the hidden curriculum in most schools, and it is taught so many ways, by teachers and other students alike. Here are a few examples of the hidden lessons I learned about gender in my school:

- In all my primary school years, all the girls in the class needed to sit at a table together. Each class had nine girls in it, but our lunch tables only sat eight. Rather than encouraging us to become friends with the boys, the teachers allowed us to move an additional chair to our table.
- In gym class, when the boys played all manner of games, the girls would usually walk laps around the track to talk or gossip. While everyone had free choice of which activity they chose, there was often judgment from other students for picking the "wrong" activity.
- In my middle school, I learned that the boys' bathrooms were expected to always be in a disgusting state, because boys were inherently gross and unclean while girls needed to be neat and well-presented.
- In high school, I learned that a boy and a girl could not be friends without eventually dating or one of them secretly having a crush on the other.

For LGBTQ+ youth, especially trans kids, these situations can all be a minefield. Who are they supposed to be friends with? Where are they supposed to eat lunch? How should they present themselves? In addition to trying to navigate hypergendered spaces, they also may have to deal with helping their peers learn to see and treat them as they are.

IDENTIFYING YOUR CHAMPIONS

Some people are fortunate to be in schools that have had trans students before and are confidently set up to support those students structurally and culturally. Others are in schools where they may be the first trans student that the school knows of, ever. Most schools fall somewhere in between: They have begun to develop those support systems but still have a way to go.

In my own experience—and that of all the people I interviewed for this book—there was often one person or one small group of people who weren't just allies: they were champions. Champions go above and beyond in regularly going to bat for their students—both helping them navigate unsupportive structures and fighting to get those structures changed. In one interview, Wallace, a nonbinary transmasculine person, shared that there was only one gender-neutral bathroom in the whole school that was safe for him to use, but a champion English teacher had the keys to a single-use staff bathroom that he let Wallace use whenever he needed. Champions aren't just faculty and staff, either; the friend I shared about earlier in the book who corrected all the other students about my name and pronouns was a champion too.

As another example, many schools tell students that their record-keeping system does not allow for name changes if the student hasn't changed their name legally. From what I have seen, heard, and learned of the technology, it is always possible to find a way to change the name or add a note in a student's profile that they want to be called something other than what's in there. It just takes a champion to decide to override arbitrary school policies and make that change.

Here are a few ways your VIP might be able to tell if someone might be a champion, whether they're teachers, administrators, guidance counselors, or others:

- Faculty leaders of the student LGBTQ+ organizations
- Faculty who are openly LGBTQ+
- Faculty who have rainbow flags or "safe zone/safe space" stickers on their classroom doors
- Faculty who normalize pronoun sharing or indicate allyship in other ways
- Faculty who have already developed a trusting relationship with your VIP who might become champions

There is also an unfortunate possibility that your VIP might not have a champion directly in their school, and depending on your relationship to them, you may need to step in and be that champion for them. Whether it is through sharing relevant legal information with your VIP about their rights in school or calling the school directly to encourage them to support your VIP, there are many ways you can be a champion for them here.

There are many resources to encourage your VIP to seek out, and if they don't exist, it's worth reaching out to their school to apply pressure to them to develop these resources.

- A student LGBTQ+ group (often called a gay-straight alliance or a gender and sexuality alliance) can offer faculty mentorship, connections with LGBTQ+ and ally peers, and a safe space to talk about their identity and challenges.
- The nurse's office or administrative office likely has at least one single-stall or gender-neutral bathroom that your VIP can use.
- The guidance counselor or social worker hopefully will have resources for students and their families on mental health, healthcare, local community resources, and strategies for families to support their VIPs.

COMING OUT AT SCHOOL

For a young person, coming out at school can feel like a tremendous undertaking, and it should be customized for your VIP specifically. Your goal is to work together with the school and your VIP to create a coming-out plan that helps them feel seen and respected as they are, from both a structural and cultural perspective.

As an example of making sure your VIP is getting support through both perspectives, consider the topic of bathrooms. Structurally, we want your VIP to have access to a bathroom that makes them feel safe and affirmed—whether that's making sure the gender-neutral bathroom is always unlocked for them or making sure the policy allows them to use the bathroom that aligns with their identity. Culturally, we want to know they aren't going to face stigma or bullying for using whichever bathroom they choose. A strong coming-out and support plan will factor in creating the necessary structural and cultural change together.

As we did in chapter 4, rather than sharing what I think your coming-out plan should be, here I will pose a list of questions for you to talk through with your VIP, and eventually with their school, to create a comprehensive plan that works for them.

Understanding the Context

You want to start by setting the scene and making sure you know what the environment you're working with is like.

1. Are there other transgender students that your VIP knows of? What about LGBTQ+ people overall? How did their coming out go?
2. Does the school have established policies/procedures for supporting transgender students?
3. Who are the teachers and students that your VIP knows/thinks will be a champion for them?
4. Who are the teachers and students your VIP is specifically worried about having negative reactions? Are any of these concerns safety related?
5. What resources does the school have already?
6. If you are not their parent, is it safe for their parents to know this is happening? If you're reading this as a teacher or administrator, know that not every state requires you to tell a student's parents you are beginning this process and that doing so may put them at risk for serious harm. You should not tell the student's parents unless *absolutely*

necessary, especially if the student has communicated to you that they have concerns for their safety.

Dreaming Big

Now that you know where you're starting from, work with your VIP to develop a plan specific to their needs and desires. There will likely be other questions specific to their age and school, but these are the key topic areas to think through as part of the plan:

1. What name and pronouns do they want their teachers and peers to call them?
   - If they're coming out in the middle of the school year, it can be a good idea to have someone reach out to their teacher/teachers directly to talk through the name change with them and ask for their assistance reminding other students of this change.
   - Where does their name show up in school records, and where is it able to be changed? Student IDs and email addresses should be easy, and schools should seek support with transcripts or official documents.
2. How do they want the news to be communicated? Would they like to share it themselves? Would they like it to be shared just with their class/classes or with the entire grade or school?
   - It is important that you get specific information from your VIP about who they are and are not comfortable sharing their identity with, and particularly whether their parents or guardians know.
3. How would they like questions to be answered? Do they want questions to be directed to themselves, or would they like to designate an ally in the school to help answer questions?
   - If you don't work at the school, this may be an opportunity for you to share additional resources with the school to help educate the staff and students so your VIP doesn't have to.
4. What would affirming participation in athletics and physical education look like for your VIP?
   - As I am writing this book, this is an extremely hot topic. There is a lot of misinformation around youth participation in sports, but if

they want to participate, sports are known for being an excellent emotional outlet and community-building space. Unfortunately, their access to sports will be very different depending on what state you're in. Know your VIP's rights and help advocate for them to participate in sports if they wish.

5. What restroom and locker room would your VIP like to use? Would they prefer access to a private space?
   - It is important to note that private accommodations should be made in a way that avoids stigmatizing the student or making them feel "othered." Many trans people end up having a supply closet as their changing room, which can feel isolating at best and dehumanizing at worst.
6. What do they want to wear to school? If there is a uniform, what options do they have that make them the most comfortable?
7. Do they know who they should go to with any concerns of bullying or harassment? Are staff members equipped to step in and support them if these situations arise?

The Bigger Picture

Your VIP's coming out is a great opportunity to review further parts of the school experience to make it as inclusive as possible for all students. Consider the following:

1. Does the school's curriculum include representation of LGBTQ+ identities?
   - Are there any books in English class with LGBTQ+ characters or authors? Are LBGTQ+ historical figures discussed in history classes?
   - Is the health/sex education curriculum inclusive of LGBTQ+ identities and relationships?
2. Are there other policies that needlessly create gender division, like specific colors of cap and gown at graduation, school uniforms, or yearbook photo outfits?
   - What policies exist that are in no way related to the students' learning or safe learning environment?

As you go through this process, check in regularly with your VIP about how things are going at school and what work they're taking on as the school learns how to support them. It is important that they know they can come to you to share uncomfortable or unsafe situations that may arise with peers or staff and to ask for your support as needed. If your VIP starts regularly missing school or has declining grades, this is likely due to challenges in mental health or a lack of support, and it's worth checking in with them to see what additional support or resources you may be able to provide.

If you are a parent or family member specifically, remember that school is not the only place they spend their time and that having a safe and welcoming home environment can be incredibly grounding as your VIP goes through a period of stress and instability at school. Hopefully, your VIP's school is willing to work with you, but remember that you have the option to seek legal assistance or support from organizations like GLSEN and the ACLU if needed. Sometimes moving to a new school allows the student to start over with other students who do not know about their transgender identity; this can be helpful if the situation at school becomes unsustainable. The important thing is to listen to your VIP and follow their lead; they'll tell you what they need to feel set up for success.

12

ACCESSING HEALTHCARE AS A TRANSGENDER PERSON

While conversations around transition-related care (as we discussed in chapter 8) dominate our conversations around gender-affirming healthcare, it's important to remember that just like everyone else, transgender people also need to go to the doctor for a variety of reactive and proactive measures: annual checkups, dental appointments, eye exams, the whole shebang.

Typically, when I speak about gender-affirming care, the assumption people make is that I'm referring to medical transition, and that's certainly part of it. But gender-affirming care is far more expansive than just top surgery or hormone therapy. Any healthcare professional who sees and treats me as I am is providing gender-affirming care. This includes my primary care provider knowing that my risk profile is different than someone else assigned female at birth because I'm on HRT, my OB-GYN using gender-neutral language to help me feel less uncomfortable during routine exams, and the patient coordinator at any healthcare office using the right name and pronouns when I check in, to name a few examples.

Because all healthcare is gender-affirming care, that means that all healthcare also has the opportunity to be specifically gender *un*affirming, and there is an unfortunate history of this being the case in many healthcare spaces. It can be challenging to find supportive providers and to know how to advocate for your VIP in those settings, so this chapter will lay out several facts and strategies to have on your mind as you go about searching for gender-affirming care.

WHAT IS "TRANS BROKEN ARM"?

Picture this: A transgender person is walking down the street and they trip and break their arm. It hurts, and they decide to go to the emergency room. When the doctor looks at their chart, they see that they have a transgender patient with a broken arm and they say, "I'm so sorry, I'm not comfortable or able to treat a transgender arm." The transgender patient says, "It's just a normal arm!" But the doctor says, "I'm going to have to ask you to leave."

This unfortunate anecdote describes a well-researched phenomenon called "transgender broken arm syndrome."[1] This phenomenon refers to the fact that many healthcare providers assume there are significant differences between transgender and cisgender bodies, feel they are unqualified or uncomfortable giving care relating to trans bodies, and refuse to care for transgender patients. There's nothing transgender about my arm—it's just a normal arm—and yet I'm at a much higher risk of being turned away from care.

So what can you do about this? If you are face-to-face with a provider who says they are unable to provide care to your VIP because of their trans identity, depending on what the type of care it is, explain to them that there is nothing that differentiates that part of the body in transgender and cisgender people and they can just treat them like a normal patient. While it varies between states, it is also important to know your VIP's legal rights. Some states have laws allowing providers to refuse to treat patients that go against their "sincerely held religious beliefs," while others have specific protections in place for transgender patients. These laws are often evolving, but Lambda Legal is an excellent resource to help you learn your VIP's rights, stay up to date about the relevant laws in your area, and find legal recourse if those rights or laws are violated.

In the long term, there is a national effort to increase healthcare provider education and fight discriminatory healthcare legislation, but in the short term, your VIP may need medical care today and you don't have time to wait. Here are a number of ways you can screen healthcare offices to help you gauge whether a medical provider is affirming:

- Call ahead and say, "Hello! I'm calling on behalf of a potential patient at your clinic/hospital/center. Is this provider knowledgeable and comfortable with treating transgender patients? Is there a specific provider who *is* knowledgeable about this kind of care that I can speak to?" While you may not get a full or perfect sense from this question, it will help weed out providers who are extremely unsupportive and potentially dangerous.

- Reach out to local LGBTQ+ organizations or groups to ask what recommendations they have, and post in local LGBTQ+ Facebook groups to ask for recommendations or find out about personal experience people may have with certain providers or centers.

- If you are already seeing a provider who is respectful, knowledgeable, and trustworthy, ask them who else in their network they trust. Often providers who are passionate about supporting transgender patients know each other well and share referrals.

- Look for small details in paperwork, such as a space to share pronouns or a preferred name that differs from a legal name. These are indications that they have put thought and effort into implementing best practices for trans care.

You may also have current providers you know and trust who also could do a better job of supporting your VIP and other trans folks that come through their office. Here are a few suggestions or requests you can make to help those providers become even more affirming:

- Suggest they update their forms to include pronouns and preferred names.

- Suggest that providers and staff have pronouns on their name badges or routinely share their pronouns on entering a patient room.

- Encourage them to hire a professional to conduct inclusive care training for the staff, including both the medical providers and the front desk team.

- If they work for a large company or hospital system, ask them to advocate for inclusion training for the providers and behind-the-scenes medical team.

- Make specific requests based on your VIP's needs.

While these are great questions to ask and suggestions to make, there's no guarantee that every medical environment will be a safe and affirming one, and it's important to talk to your VIP about how to advocate for themselves in medical settings. Again, these are problems that in the long term we are fighting at their sources, but when you're already in that provider's office, you don't have time to wait for an updated medical school curriculum to make its way to this specific doctor. The following are a few recommendations for how to get through these situations as safely as possible.

Stay Informed

One of the most common challenges trans folks face in medical settings is providers who may not know as much about our care as they should due to a lack of trans-inclusive medical education. Providers who are trans affirming become that way because they choose to put in the time and resources to do so. If you know your VIP has an appointment scheduled at the OB-GYN or with a primary care provider or GI doctor, spend some time researching "considerations for OB-GYN care for transgender men." Groups like Fenway Health, UCSF Health, WPATH, and the Mayo Clinic are often at the forefront of trans health research and will likely have the most up-to-date information on their websites. You don't need to have a perfect understanding of the medical literature (I know I don't), but it will help to have some general information to bring should you need to remind your provider that there are certain tests they forgot to run or questions they forgot to ask. If you're concerned about getting pushback on specific questions or requests from your doctor, consider bringing physical copies of studies or web pages with evidence that you can share with them.

Ask for Clarity

Another common challenge is healthcare providers asking questions that are invasive or overly personal. I've been asked a wide variety of wholly irrelevant questions by people in medical settings. It's important to understand that there's a difference between questions that are invasive and questions that are a *necessary* type of awkward. When I am in a healthcare setting and I'm asked a question that falls somewhere on the spectrum between the two,

I ask the provider to share with me why they need that information so I can give them information that is helpful to them or explain why I won't be answering.

Say No

It can be challenging to say no to things, especially in a medical setting where there is an explicit power dynamic—your VIP needs healthcare and the provider gets to decide if they deserve it. Phrases that get across the clear message of "I don't want to answer that" without jeopardizing your VIP's access to care include "I'm not comfortable answering that" and "I don't understand how that question is relevant to the care I'm here to receive."

Plan Accordingly

Trying to keep all these things in mind means that going to the doctor is especially taxing for trans folks. On days where your VIP has a doctor's appointment, consider planning something fun or restorative directly after. Whether it's going for ice cream, playing hooky from school together, or spending time at an LGBTQ+ community center, help balance out the day with something healing when you know there are going to be challenges you can't protect them from.

SEX-SPECIFIC MEDICAL EXAMS

While we're talking about unavoidably uncomfortable medical settings, there are certain body-specific screenings your VIP will need to have throughout the course of their life.

Because many healthcare providers lack knowledge about trans care and experience about the dysphoria and discomfort that accompany these exams, many trans folks delay routine cancer screenings, including prostate exams, mammograms, and Pap tests. While it can be tempting to just avoid the discomfort by avoiding the screenings, these are critical tests for long-term health, depending on your VIP's age, and there are ways to support them in making these exams feel less challenging.

For me, calling OB-GYN care a "sore spot" would be the understatement of the century. I would stress about my appointment from the moment I scheduled it until hours or even days after the appointment. To help you understand why it might be challenging for your VIP, I'll share a list of the things I disliked about going to the OB-GYN as well as the solutions I've found to make them more tolerable:

1. Entering the physical space, which was very woman-centric, reminded me that despite any and all changes I might go through, there were parts of me that would always make others see me as a woman.
   Solution: Systemically, there is a movement to encourage a shift in language from calling gynecological care "women's health" to calling it "pelvic health," which is more descriptive and accurate. Individually, I was able to arrange appointment times where I knew I could walk quickly through the waiting room without spending too much time taking in the decoration or could otherwise bring a distraction like a book.
2. When I couldn't avoid it, sitting in the waiting room was challenging. Most people at the OB-GYN aren't expecting to see a young, unaccompanied man sitting across from them in the OB-GYN office, and I was frequently on the receiving end of stares that reminded me how out of place I was.
   Solution: My mom was able to arrange for me to be the first appointment of the day so I didn't need to share the waiting room with anyone, and when I left I was given the option of using a side door that didn't take me out through the then-crowded room.
3. Unfortunately, I have had OB-GYNs in the past who were not the most knowledgeable about transgender health, and as a result I didn't receive adequate care. From sharing my concerns about hormonal birth control to asking questions about the gynecological effects of going on testosterone, I was brushed off and felt I couldn't ask my OB-GYN questions about things that later became serious medical issues.
   Solution: I'm very fortunate that St. Louis, where I live now, has an exceptional center for transgender health that includes OB-GYNs specifically trained and focusing on transgender patients. The office lacks gender-specific decorations, and the doctor's care is well informed

to suit the trans population. If possible, I encourage you to seek out centers like this one in your nearest major metropolitan area. If you don't have a center nearby, the "call ahead" or other research methods mentioned earlier will be your best tool here, as there are often smaller practices that are designed to be similarly affirming.

4. Receiving gynecological care is a source of dysphoria for me. At the end of the day, no matter how many precautions are in place, no matter how kind or respectful the provider is, I'm still going to need to be aware of that part of my body for gynecological exams, and it's really uncomfortable and dysphoria inducing for me.

Solution: Of all the problems I mentioned, this one is the least "solvable." There's no one doing anything *wrong* here; I just don't like going to the OB-GYN. For me, self-care in this instance might look like asking my wife to come with me and keep me distracted or planning something fun directly afterward that I can spend the time looking forward to instead of dreading the appointment.

This list doesn't capture everything that could possibly make a person uncomfortable, but it does highlight many of the key points, which is to help your VIP determine what their needs are and advocate for those needs.

13

LEAVING THE NEST

Preparing Your VIP for College, the Workforce, and the World

Depending on your VIP's age, one of the scariest things about support-ing them is knowing there's only so much you can do to kep them safe when they go out into the world. In this chapter, we're going to talk through a few strategies and things to know on a broad level about the different places your VIP might be heading—whether it is the workplace, college, or just a new city—how to support them in those spaces, and what you should know about helping them finding safe and inclusive places to be.

In general, when I think about determining whether a company, college, or city is an inclusive space, the biggest things I look for are intentionality and resources.

With intentionality, I'm looking for places and people that have put time and thought into implementing best-practice inclusion principles. As an example, I strongly encourage people not to apply for a job or college if the application doesn't include a space for pronouns. This isn't because I care *so* strongly about the sharing of pronouns—though I do think it's great—but be-cause at this point, sharing your pronouns is a widely understood way to be an inclusive community that requires minimal effort and has minimal impact outside of allyship. When an application doesn't ask for my pronouns, it in-dicates to me that either they are at a very early stage of their allyship journey or they view that surface-level commitment as "too much" and likely haven't or won't put time into other inclusion initiatives that require more effort.

In terms of resources, I look for proof that a group sees it as worthwhile to invest significant resources in inclusivity—even if the resources aren't things that directly benefit me, it indicates to me that they view the trans community as worthy of support. As an example, I look for gender-neutral bathrooms on college campuses and at workplaces even though I am most comfortable in the men's room. Like pronouns, providing gender-neutral bathrooms is a well-known practice for including trans and nonbinary people in physical spaces, though they require much more effort to implement. If an organization has been willing to invest in creating gender-neutral bathrooms, they're also more likely to invest resources into supporting your VIP and to stand by their side should an instance of transphobia or discrimination arise.

While I am against virtue-signaling—the idea that people will do certain things *only* to send the message that they're the best ally—as a concept, I do think there are a variety of tangible commitments that workplaces, colleges, and cities can make that send a clear message of support, and we'll talk through how to look for those messages.

As your VIP gets older, they are going to be increasingly independent in their choices and may not seek as much direct guidance from you on these topics. That said, I want to touch on them briefly to help ease your concerns and frame the guidance you *do* give them.

COLLEGE

So your VIP is thinking about heading to college, something that often carries with it a combination of excitement and stress. In addition to all the typical stressors of the college application process, your VIP has the additional layer of worrying about finding a place that will be safe and affirming of their identity. In general, there are a few best practices for searching for welcoming campuses. A number of guides are available online, and those are great places to start, but I found that doing my own research helped me feel more secure in a decision as big as this one.

When looking at colleges, here are a few things to consider:

1. *Are there gender-neutral bathrooms?* At most colleges, new buildings are always in the works, and not including gender-neutral bathrooms

in a new design is an intentional choice toward exclusion. When I arrived for campus visits, I asked the admissions officers where the gender-neutral bathrooms were on campus. If they didn't know of any or there were only a handful located in a basement, that was a huge red flag to me.

2. *Is there an LGBTQ+ student center? Is there a full- or part-time staff member running the center and supporting LGBTQ+ students?* Even if your VIP doesn't specifically want to hang out at the student center, the presence of one indicates that the college is proactively investing resources into supporting the trans and queer community.

3. *Is there a current trans student your VIP can talk to?* This was one of the most helpful tools in my decision-making toolkit. I either asked admissions directly, found the LGBTQ+ student center staff member's email, or reached out to the LGBTQ+ student group's page on social media. Once in contact with a current trans student, I was able to ask more about what it was like, what support they found, and what challenges they faced. They were generally extremely honest with me about whether they would have picked their school again given the choice.

4. *What name does the college use for your VIP in mail and email communications?* While most applications give you an opportunity to share a preferred name that is not your legal name, not all schools will *use* that preferred name. I found that some schools took care to make sure everything was addressed correctly and adjusted the systems that collected and used name data, other schools hadn't adjusted their systems but allegedly began the process as soon as I reached out to ask for the correct name on my communications, and some schools simply told me it was their policy to use the legal name of their applicants. If a school doesn't get it right in the communications stage, there is a high likelihood it may be a problem with things like class rosters and diplomas. It is also, again, a signal that they do or do not see it as worthwhile to invest in creating more inclusive structures.

5. *What is the college's housing policy?* There are a variety of best practices for how to run trans-inclusive student housing, and there are also a variety of preferences different people might have that will make them feel the safest. I went to Brandeis, and all the trans students were

reached out to for one-on-one meetings to talk about their options. We could request a single room; we could request a same-gender roommate, a same-sex roommate, or another trans student roommate; or we could pick our own roommate, even though most other students did not have that option. Your best bet will be a college with *options* rather than a one-size-fits-all solution.

6. *What state is the college in?* Unfortunately, given the state of anti-LGBTQ+ legislation across the country, your VIP does need to consider which states have laws protecting them from discrimination and transphobia and which states are actively making it worse. While not every law will impact your VIP directly, existing laws continue to build on each other and feed a general culture of hatred and fear around the trans community that may make it less safe to leave campus.

The good news is that colleges are known for being extremely diverse and full of passionate students who are eager to make a difference, and even if your VIP ends up choosing a school that isn't perfect, they likely won't be alone in fighting to improve the school for themselves and the trans folks that come after them.

FINDING A SAFE AND SUPPORTIVE WORKPLACE

If your VIP is beginning a job search, an already tedious process, it can be easy to overlook the important considerations in finding a workplace that will see and treat them respectfully. No policy the company shares is a 100 percent guarantee that they're a supportive environment, but the more positive answers, the more comfortable your VIP will likely be going into that unknown situation. Not all of these questions will apply in every workplace, and there may be differences between blue-collar and white-collar jobs or between large and small companies, but it's important to help your VIP determine which of these questions are the most significant to them.

Here are a few questions to guide your research:

1. *Does the company celebrate pride month?* This isn't just asking whether a company slapped a rainbow logo on their Facebook page on June 1;

it's also asking if it honored their LGBTQ+ employees publicly, if it put on educational and celebratory events, if it made any charitable donations, and if it marched in or sponsored a pride parade. What level of visible allyship is the company comfortable with, and is it willing to stand up to backlash?

2. *Does the company have inclusive policies?* The landscape of best practice policies is always evolving, but there are certain policies that are part of a very solid foundation of support. Remember again that these policies don't all need to directly impact you; we are just looking for a pattern of commitment to inclusivity. Best practice policies might be things like:

• Pronoun-sharing policies
• Inclusive and equitable parental leave
• A strong nondiscrimination policy that is enforced
• A gender transition policy, which indicates the company has had trans employees before
• Relocation plans for folks living in unsafe states or healthcare stipends for traveling for healthcare access

3. *Does the company have employee resource groups?* Whether they're called employee resource groups (ERGs) business resource groups (BRGs), affinity groups, or something else, having a group of LGBTQ+ and ally employees indicates that there are plenty of other visible queer folks or allies at the company and that it is willing to invest resources in this community.

4. *Does the company's health insurance cover transition-related care?* Gender-affirming care is expensive, especially without insurance, and not every insurance provider covers gender-affirming care. There are other parts of the queer experience that might be covered, like IVF, adoption costs, and voice therapy. Does it cover mental health care as well?

5. *If it's a larger company, is it scored on the Human Rights Campaign's Corporate Equality Index?* The Human Rights Campaign is a major national organization that has developed a multifaceted assessment for a company's LGBTQ+ inclusion policies and practices. While it's not a perfect assessment, it's a great data point.

It is also important that your VIP knows their legal rights in the workplace, as there are certain things that are and are not permissible depending on the state they're in. Given how constantly the legal landscape is changing, it is important to consult national legal protection resource sharing pages that are as up to date as possible and to research this information for your own state as well. Lambda Legal, the ACLU, or the Transgender Legal Defense Fund are great resources for this.

DATING AND RELATIONSHIPS

Your VIP might not be interested in dating at all—sometimes people identify as asexual or aromantic, meaning that they don't experience sexual or romantic attraction. These identities are not a deficit or a sentence for an unfulfilled life; they just mean that sex or romance (depending on their identity) isn't a top priority or a requirement for life to feel fulfilling. While dating is a sphere you may not be able to help as much with, I want to share some answers to common questions about dating to help quell any concerns you might have about your VIP's future.

- Can transgender people date?
  Yes! While there might be some additional challenges at play, transgender people can date and love like anyone else if they'd like to.
- Can trans people date cisgender people, or do they only date other transgender people?
  Trans people can date anyone they want (who also wants to date them back, obviously), though some trans folks might choose only to date other transgender people to avoid needing to explain their identity to new partners.
- Can transgender people have kids?
  Yes! Some trans folks assigned female at birth will choose to carry a child—and researchers are currently in the process of developing womb transplants for cisgender women and trans women alike! There is still developing research about the effects of hormone replacement therapy on fertility, but this is a great question for your VIP's doctor if they're interested in learning more. Alternatively, trans families can

also choose to get a surrogate or adopt a child. There are so many ways a family can be configured, and none are more "real" than any others.

- Does a transgender person need to tell their partner right away that they are transgender?

This is a hotly debated topic, and while a trans person will likely need to tell their partner *eventually* if they date long enough, many people feel that disclosing a trans identity too soon isn't a good idea. Dating is about getting to know someone, and a trans person's gender identity just one part of their story.

- Why do some queer relationships move so fast?

This doesn't apply to *every* queer relationship, but LGBTQ+ relationships often move "faster" than typical straight relationships. There are many reasons for this, one of which is that LGBTQ+ people are typically very open with their emotions and vulnerability, so there is less "breaking the ice" time required than in other relationships. The speed a relationship moves is neither good nor bad (generally), if your VIP is truly happy and safe.

These lessons about moving into the world as a trans adult are ones your VIP has to learn from the world around them, from their own experiences and misadventures, and from the community they will continue to build around them. If you're showing up as a proud ally, this community is likely going to include you, but you will be just one part of a much broader support network.

You aren't going to be able to guide your VIP through every issue, protect them from every threat, or answer every question. The older they get, the bigger the challenges they will face, but they will grow and rise to the challenge, and you'll be there to lift them up whenever they fall and be the wind beneath their wings when and where you can. If you're wondering how else you can be an ally to your VIP after they're grown, many of the tips in this book still apply. The most important tip I have remains the most important into adulthood: Listen to your VIP. I can't tell you what they need, but they can. They will show you the way.

14

BIGGER THAN US

Supporting Trans Youth around the Country

Up until now, we've focused a lot on how to show up for your VIP—and indeed, a lot of the most important allyship happens on an interpersonal level—but I want to close this book out by reminding you that *things don't have to be this way.* So many of the strategies we've talked through, while helpful, are backdoors around unsupportive structures or skills for surviving in unsupportive environments, and our longer-term goal should be to create a world that is supportive by default.

While it can be easy to fall into hopelessness, and it can feel like this issue is irredeemably polarized, this fight is far from over (depending on when you're reading this, I suppose). When I got into public speaking, I accepted that my new reality was spending my days toe to toe with people who hated me—I was ready for backlash, offensive statements, and hecklers. Instead, I found a country of people who were full of questions and confusion but felt afraid to ask the wrong thing. In my educational and advocacy work, I have spoken with countless individuals who genuinely changed their perspectives and decided to become allies. Over these years, I have seen politicians change their platforms (or be defeated in courts and elections). I have met people in huge cities and the tiniest towns, of all manner of backgrounds, who are ready, willing, and able to advocate passionately for the trans community.

All this is to say that advocacy makes a real difference. In my work as an activist regularly speaking with news outlets and traveling to the Missouri capitol, the people I see showing up the most often are the parents and loved ones of trans kids who are passionate supporters of their VIPS, and their stories are having a huge impact on politicians, on people learning about these issues, and on the way local and national media talk about the hateful bills making their way through state legislatures.

While you do not *have* to get involved, your VIP is almost certainly acutely aware and afraid of the hateful legislation spreading across the country, and taking the weight of fighting back onto your own shoulders is an extremely powerful way to show love and true allyship.

There are a wide variety of ways to get involved in social movements beyond being on the front lines of a protest or testifying in front of legislators, many of which are wonderful things for your whole family to do together. In addition to staying informed about the state of anti-trans legislation through wonderful resources like Erin Reed's Substack *Erin in the Morning*, it's important to find a role that matches your skills and that you find enjoyable. This is a marathon, not a sprint, and we want our work to be both impactful and sustainable.

From where I stand, I see four key categories of roles/skills in social movements, and many people have a mix of skills from each of these categories or fill different roles in different spaces. There is no "ranking" of the roles, and you should focus on getting involved in a way that feels authentic and sustainable to you.

THE ORGANIZER

The organizer is the first type of person who likely comes to mind when you think of political involvement. The organizer is efficient, effective, and a strong leader. They know the answer to 90 percent of the questions you ask and know exactly who to call for the other 10 percent.

Here are a few ways the organizer helps lead social movements:

- Planning meetings, rallies, or protests
- Keeping the community up to date about important news updates
- Determining the areas of greatest financial need and directing donations toward them

- Creating rapid-response strategies and strategic long-term plans
- Helping individuals newer to the movement decide how to get involved

There may be certain areas where you are more knowledgeable than others. I am an organizer in Missouri politics, for example, but am much less of a knowledge leader when it comes to national or international politics. It is okay to fill different roles in different spaces; what matters is that we speak up when we're knowledgeable and able and make time to listen when others have things to teach.

If you're early in your political journey but would like to leverage your knowledge or expertise in this realm, here are some suggestions for ways you might begin to get involved:

- As challenges come up in your local political sphere, contact connections you have that might be able to be allies or sources of information, such as city officials, congressional staffers, or law firms, and ask them to consider supporting the organizations leading the community response.
- If there are projects underway that you know you have skills to contribute to or that remind you of projects you've been successfully involved in, reach out to someone affiliated with the project and offer them your specific skills or background.
- Sign up for news updates from your state and local LGBTQ+ groups to stay as informed as possible, and share helpful information with other people you know.
- When you hear about calls to action from your local leaders, organize people in your life and community to follow those calls.

THE SPEAKER

The speaker is one of the voices and faces of the movement. You're most likely to find them in front of a crowd, whether on purpose or by accident, and they're likely to be the one you call when you need a top-tier pep talk.

Here are some of the ways speakers lead:

- Testifying at legislative hearings
- Sharing their story with reporters for written and filmed news stories

- Speaking at rallies and protests
- Helping create public-facing statements to respond to current events

One thing that's important to highlight about the speaker role is that while certain areas do require substantial expertise, I find that storytelling has the greatest potential for positive impact on the hearts and minds we're trying to change. Simply sharing your lived experience and your knowledge of and love for your VIP will have a major impact on the people who see it. It's also important to know what you are and aren't knowledgeable about. For example, I know that I don't have medical credentials, so I refrain from positioning myself as an expert on the science of gender-affirming care; instead, I focus on my own story of gender-affirming care and my expertise in understanding the human impact and broader implications of gender-affirming care.

If you'd like to get more involved as a speaker, here are a few ways to get started:

- Sign up to testify at a legislative hearing and reach out to your local LGBTQ+ organization to ask for some assistance in preparing your testimony.
- Research communication guidance for the specific issues you're hoping to speak to, as there are certain talking points we have found to be least and most effective over time. Organizations like the Movement Advancement Project have developed a number of messaging guides that may be helpful.
- Reach out to local and national LGBTQ+ organizations to see if any of them offer media trainings for people interested in sharing their story with journalists.
- Research videos of legislative testimony from people with similar connections to the movement as you and take note of what elements of their testimony you find most powerful.

THE CARETAKER

As I mentioned earlier, this movement is a marathon and not a sprint. This means we need to make sure our people are taken care of and lifted up, and that's the role of the caretaker.

Here are a few ways the caretaker can show up to take care of others who are on the front lines:

- Preparing food for individuals who may have spent all day lobbying or who might enjoy surprise baked goods
- Holding space for people to vent their frustrations, cry, be angry, or anything else; this might look like talking about it, but it might also look like just having an open door, a hot cup of tea, and a pile of blankets
- Donating money or providing other resources like transportation or gender-affirming clothing
- Planning joyful or healing gathering events to build a sense of community in challenging times
- Allowing folks from different parts of the state to use their guest room to travel affordably for cross-state advocacy

Specifically when working as a caretaker in trans advocacy spaces, you're likely to be side by side with many trans activists who may not have access to supportive parents or adult figures in their lives, and depending on your skills and positionality, there are additional ways you might show up for them:

- Act as a substitute parent or family member for holidays, home-cooked meals, and emotional support.
- Share information that is typically passed down generationally such as home maintenance skills, cleaning skills, cooking skills, or financial literacy.
- Offer "free mom hugs" or "free dad hugs."

And don't forget: as a caretaker you will also need (and deserve) to be taken care of!

THE CONVERSATIONALIST

The conversationalist is a lesser-known role, but in my opinion, it is one of the most important. While social media and news out of state capitols may make it feel like everyone has an extremely strong, extremely polarized opinion about these topics, according to a wide range of bipartisan polling, most of the country doesn't understand much of what's going and doesn't quite know how to feel about it. These are the hearts and minds that we are likely to be able to reach. The conversationalist talks to their coworkers, family members, fellow religious congregants, and neighbors about what's going on and breaks down some of the misinformation they're likely to have heard.

Here are some ways conversationalists advocate for trans people:

- Interrupting casually transphobic jokes or comments
- Gently correcting misinformation when it comes up in conversation
- Being a trustworthy resource for questions people might feel embarrassed to ask
- Making sure that those around them understand the gravity and the aggression of the increase in transphobia

The conversationalist role is crucial because trans exclusion has become a "hot policy" that many conservatives believe will get them votes. By changing the minds of people in their districts, we send the message that these policies are not popular, and the politicians will have no choice but to change their stance.

If you're hoping to get involved as a conversationalist, here are some ways to start:

- Research messaging guidance for topics you're hoping to talk about with others to make sure you have all the facts.
- Practice answering questions with friends and family members you know are very likely to be supportive.
- Attend a parent support group meeting and offer words of support or guidance to other parents.
- Strike up conversations with members of your community, whether it's by asking if they have any questions about what's been going on or just asking them for their thoughts on some of the anti-trans bills in your area.

One thing that's crucial to remember as a conversationalist is that it's okay to not be 100 percent knowledgeable about every topic; if anything, it makes a positive impact to demonstrate to others that it's okay to have questions. I am always happy to be asked a question I don't know the answer to. It makes the folks I'm talking to feel like it isn't "too late" for them to start learning, and it allows me to share the strategies I use for finding good answers to questions I have.

SAFETY IN ADVOCACY

When thinking about political activism, it's crucial to have safety on your radar, both for yourself and for your VIP. The unfortunate reality is that being visible trans people can put a target on our backs, and as the saying goes, "If you're trying to be my ally and the stones thrown at me aren't hitting you, you aren't standing close enough." Showing up wholeheartedly for your VIP means that there are going to be people who don't like you and who may want to find a way to let you know that.

If you are going to certain protests or rallies it's important to learn what the safety plan is for the rally and if significant counterprotestor presence is expected. It may not always be safe for your VIP to attend if there are likely to be arrests or clashes with opposition. Especially if your VIP is younger, not every rally or march will be appropriate or safe for them. If you are ever in doubt, reach out to the organizers of the event to ask whether it's a good idea to bring your VIP.

While the landscape of physical safety is likely to continue to evolve over time, one of the most timeless tips I can give you if you're going to share your name and story publicly is to investigate data privacy upgrades. Because of the way technology is set up right now, most of your personal information (address, phone number, etc.) is available for sale through a variety of data brokers. I use a website called Delete Me (joindeleteme.com) to make sure that trolls, or anyone else who may not wish me well, cannot access any of my identifying information.

Beyond physical safety, it is important to consider psychological safety. When I go to testify at the Missouri capitol, I often come home drained. After my first trip, I couldn't sleep for days because I kept hearing the vile words the senators spoke in my head. You should be aware that some of the people who oppose us are *truly* cruel, and will say things a young person should not be hearing. While a trans youth coming to testify can be extremely powerful for those listening, the experience can be extremely traumatic for the youth themselves. Going to beg for your rights and being met with legislators who are on their phones, laughing at you, or asking you questions about your genitals (yes, really), can be a struggle to process and recover from, even as an adult who has spent nearly a decade living as a transgender person.

This isn't a decision I can make for you, nor is it a decision you can make on behalf of your VIP, but it's important they know what they're walking into and have ample space set up to process, heal, or grieve afterward.

WHAT IS "ENOUGH"?

Sometimes I catch myself feeling like I'm not doing enough. Whether it's because I chose not to attend a hearing, or missed out on an action item because I was taking a break from social media, I feel guilty about what I'm *not* doing.

Most of my entire life and career are devoted to this movement. I spend most of my time doing as much as possible for the people and the movement around me, and yet I still feel like I should be doing more because things feel like they're just continuing to get worse and worse. Recently, though, I had a revelation about this concept of "doing enough": There is no such thing as "enough." One person is never, ever going to be able to do enough to fix things on their own, and that is by design. The people who are against us are clever, powerful, and well resourced—of course it's going to take *all of us* to fight back. You will never be able to do enough on your own, which also means that when you do as much as you can, it *is* enough.

I'm not saying that sitting back and sharing one Facebook post is enough because "anything is enough." What I'm saying is that doing everything that you reasonably can, while keeping it authentic and sustainable, is enough.

Building a better world for our VIPs—and for everyone out there who doesn't have an incredible ally reading this book and deciding to show up for them—is going to take every single one of us, but I am confident that with every single one of us, we will be able to make that world a reality.

CONCLUSION

Well, reader, we made it. To where, exactly, I don't know. This part is called the conclusion, but I think you and I both know that nothing is actually concluding; this section is just called the conclusion because that's what my publisher told me it was supposed to be called.

I hope this book has left you feeling ready to go into the world as a good ally—not a perfect one, because there is no such thing, but a truly *good* ally to your VIP and to the trans community as a whole. Remember, allyship is a lifelong journey of learning, supporting, making mistakes, growing from those mistakes, making different mistakes, and growing from those ones too. In my work as both an advocate for myself and a passionate ally for other marginalized groups, I hold tight to my motto: "All I can do is be even better tomorrow." I know that today I'm doing the best I can with the information I have, and I know that I might get called out for doing something wrong or learn something new that I didn't know before, and that will give me the skills to be an even better person tomorrow. I don't expect to automatically know, understand, or remember every fact, but I do my best to continue learning and to be grateful for opportunities to do so in whatever form that may take.

We don't get to call ourselves allies; all we can do is behave as we hope an ally would and let the people we're showing up to support determine if we're doing a good job. There may not be a medal or an award, but that's not why we do this work. We do it because we love our VIPs, because they deserve to be loved and supported by default, and because we hope that the people around us will show up with strength and compassion for us in return when we need our own allies. The fight to build a better world builds a world that is better for every single one of us.

To close out our conversation (for now), I'll leave you with this. Lately, I've seen a new question enter my list of frequently asked questions:

Knowing all you do about the hate the transgender community gets, was it worth it? If you could snap your fingers and have been born a cisgender man instead, would you?

My answer is the same every time: I will always choose to be trans. To me, it has been one of the most magical, liberating experiences of my life. Being trans means I have become my own creator, and there is something magnificent about building my own body, my own idea of masculinity, my own experience of gender and sexuality. Being trans has given me some of the most powerful self-reflection and self-awareness skills of anyone I know, and it has brought me community with so many brilliant, passionate, rule-breaking trans folks and ally champions around the world who I am so grateful for.

I would never choose to be treated the way I am by the world around me, but I would choose to create myself this way every time. Your VIP may feel the same or they may not. The way people treat us can be horrible, and that may outweigh the joy your VIP is able to find in their euphoria, but I hope with all my heart that this book, and that our work, make that pain short-lived. I feel confident that together we will win this fight and build a world where every single person gets to be celebrated because of, not in spite of, who they are.

Thank you for being on this journey with me.

Together in Power,
Ben

GLOSSARY OF TERMS

AFAB: Assigned female at birth.

Agender: Someone who does not identify as any gender.

AMAB: Assigned male at birth.

Androgynous: Someone who has a combination of both masculine and feminine characteristics.

Aromantic/Aro: Someone who does not experience romantic attraction. This can also show up on a spectrum in the same way that asexuality does. Some people never experience it, others experience it minimally, while others only feel it with people they have extremely close platonic bonds with.

Asexual/Ace: Someone who does not experience sexual attraction: some people experience it in limited amounts or only in specific situations, while others are sex repulsed. This spectrum is sometimes referred to as "gray asexual."

Bi/Bisexual: Someone who is attracted to both their own gender identity and other gender identities.

Biological Sex: The biological categories (male, female, or intersex) into which humans and most other living things are divided based on their reproductive functions.

Cisgender: Someone whose gender identity is the same as the sex they were assigned at birth.

Cisnormativity: The idea that cisgender identities are a normal/default identity and all other identities are viewed as deviations from that norm.

Drag Queen/King: Someone who uses outfit and character to perform an art piece making a statement about gender identities or gender roles. Drag artists will often dress up with gender expressions different than what they would present with in their day-to-day life.

FtM: Female-to-male.

Gay: A man who is only attracted to other men. More recently, it has become an umbrella term used by LGBTQ+ people of all gender identities and sexualities to describe themselves and/or their relationships, similar to the word "queer." It may also be as a way to take away and reclaim the power of phrases like, "That's so gay."

Gender: Someone's internal sense of being male, female, or another identity.

Gender Binary: The classification of gender into two distinct categories: man and woman.

Gender Dysphoria: A feeling of discomfort or distress due to a mismatch between someone's biological sex and their gender identity. *Physical dysphoria* refers to the type of gender dysphoria one may have about their body, while *social dysphoria* refers to the discomfort of being seen or referred to incorrectly.

Gender Euphoria: A feeling of joy and comfort when someone's gender expression is aligned with their identity.

Gender Expansive/Gender Creative: Someone whose gender identity defies current societal expectations and understandings of gender.

Gender Expression: How someone manifests their gender identity, whether it is through clothing, hairstyles, mannerisms, etc.; often classified as masculine or feminine.

Gender Fluid: Someone whose identity fluctuates over time: by the week, by the month, by the day, or even by the hour.

Gender Nonconforming: Someone whose gender presentation does not align with what is typically expected from someone of that identity.

Genderqueer: Genderqueer is an expansion of the term queer, which, as it relates to sexuality, is an umbrella term for those who have attractions that are outside of what society views as "normal." Genderqueer, in turn, is an umbrella term for a gender identity that is outside of what's viewed as "normal." In this case, "normal" being male or female.

Gender Roles: Culturally established and enforced expectations for someone's grooming, interests, career, and personality based on their gender identity.

Intersex: Someone who is born with sex characteristics outside of the typical definitions of male and female. This may look like differences in genitalia, differences in reproductive capabilities, or chromosomes outside of XX and XY. This is also increasingly being referred to as "disorders of sexual development."

Lesbian: A woman who is only attracted to other women.

LGBTQ+: An acronym that stands for lesbian, gay, bisexual, transgender, queer, and more; used to describe people whose sexualities or gender identities fall outside of what society deems "normal."

LGBTQIA+: An elongated form of the acronym often used in the United States that evolved specifically to include intersex, asexual, and aromantic people.

LGBTQIA2S+: An elongated form of the acronym most often used in Canada to specifically include Two-Spirit people.

LGBTQIA+ Community: Everyone who identifies as LGBTQIA+.

MtF: Male-to-female.

Nonbinary: Someone who does not identify as male or female. Some folks just identify as nonbinary while others use it as an umbrella term and have other labels they use as well.

Pangender: Someone who identifies as many gender identities at once.

Pansexual: Someone who is attracted to people regardless of their gender identity.

Passing: The act of being read as the correct gender identity, or of people assuming someone is cisgender. For a transgender man, for example, passing occurs when people assume I was assigned male at birth or when they use the correct pronouns and gendered language for me without asking.

Queer: This word has many different meanings for different people. For many, especially a large proportion of the youngest members of the community, the word queer is used as an umbrella term to mean any identity that is outside of what larger society views as "normal." People who feel their identities are too complex or fluid to describe to others or even to understand themselves find it a comfortable "catchall" label. The origins of this word, however, are less open and friendly. Before the 1980s, queer was used as a hateful slur against LGBTQ+ people, but as time passed and visibility and resilience increased, some members of the LGBTQ+ community began to reclaim it. The concept of reclaiming slurs is not unique to the LGBTQ+ community; many marginalized groups have taken the words used to harm them and claimed them as their own with a new, empowering meaning. By casually and lovingly using words like queer, members of the LGBTQ+ community take away the power they have over us as messages of hate. That said, some people may never be able to move past the hurtful memories the word brings up for them. To stay on the safe side, if you want to use this word to refer to someone else, it's best to check in with them about how they feel about it.

Sexuality/Sexual Orientation: Someone's identity based on the gender or gender identities to which they experience attraction.

Social Transition: Changing the way one presents and is referred to socially through changes to things like name, pronouns, wardrobe, and hair.

Transgender: Someone whose gender identity is different than the sex they were assigned at birth.

Trans man: Someone who is transitioning to male.

Trans woman: Someone who is transitioning to female.

NOTES

CHAPTER 1

1. M. H. Morton, A. Dworsky, and G. M. Samuels, "Missed Opportunities: Youth Homelessness in America. National Estimates," Voices of Youth Count, 2017, https://voicesofyouthcount.org/brief/national-estimates-of-youth-homeless ness/.

CHAPTER 5

1. Susan Silk and Barry Goldman, "Ring Theory: How Not to Say the Wrong Thing," *Los Angeles Times*, May 12, 2020, https://www.latimes.com/opinion/op-ed /la-xpm-2013-apr-07-la-oe-0407-silk-ring-theory-20130407-story.html.

2. Erin Reed, "US Internal Refugee Crisis: 130–260k Trans People Have Already Fled," *Erin in the Morning*, June 13, 2023, https://www.erininthemorning .com/p/us-internal-refugee-crisis-130-260k.

3. Strong Family Alliance, "Faith-Based Organizations," November 9, 2022, https://www.strongfamilyalliance.org/hopeful-voices/faith-based-organizations/.

4. Daniel M. Lavery, *Something That May Shock and Discredit You* (New York: Atria Books, 2020).

5. Minnesota Department of Health, "Summary of Findings: A Review of Scientific Evidence of Conversion Therapy," April 11, 2022, https://www.health.state .mn.us/people/conversiontherapy.pdf; Katie M. Heiden Rootes, Christi R. Mcgeorge,

Joanne Salas, and Samantha Levine, "The Effects of Gender Identity Change Efforts on Black, Latinx, and White Transgender and Gender Nonbinary Adults: Implications for Ethical Clinical Practice," *Journal of Marital and Family Therapy* 48, no. 3 (2021), http://dx.doi.org/10.1111/jmft.12575.

CHAPTER 6

1. Sarah E. Valentine and Jillian C. Shipherd, "A Systematic Review of Social Stress and Mental Health among Transgender and Gender Non-Conforming People in the United States," *Clinical Psychology Review* 66 (December 1, 2018): 24–38, https://doi.org/10.1016/j.cpr.2018.03.003.

CHAPTER 8

1. Brandy Schillace, "The Forgotten History of the World's First Trans Clinic," *Scientific American*, May 10, 2021, https://www.scientificamerican.com/article/the-forgotten-history-of-the-worlds-first-trans-clinic/.

2. Yacob Reyes, "Transition-Related Surgery Limited to Teens, Not 'Young Kids.' Even Then, It's Rare," PolitiFact, August 10, 2022,, https://www.politifact.com/factchecks/2022/aug/10/ron-desantis/transition-related-surgery-limited-teens-not-young/.

3. UCSF Gender Affirming Health Program, "Welcome," https://transcare.ucsf.edu/welcome-0.

4. Kellan E. Baker et al. "Hormone Therapy, Mental Health, and Quality of Life among Transgender People: A Systematic Review," *Journal of the Endocrine Society* 5, no. 4 (2021), https://doi.org/10.1210/jendso/bvab011.

5. Lindsey Tanner, "How Common Is Transgender Treatment Regret, Detransitioning?" AP News, August 18, 2023, https://apnews.com/article/transgender-treatment-regret-detransition-371e927ec6e7a24cd9c77b5371c6ba2b.

6. Jack L. Turban et al., "Factors Leading to 'Detransition' Among Transgender and Gender Diverse People in the United States: A Mixed-Methods Analysis," *LGBT Health* 8, no. 4 (June 1, 2021): 273–80, https://doi.org/10.1089/lgbt.2020.0437.

7. Diana M. Tordoff et al., "Mental Health Outcomes in Transgender and Nonbinary Youths Receiving Gender-Affirming Care," *JAMA* 5, no. 2 (February 25, 2022): e220978, https://doi.org/10.1001/jamanetworkopen.2022.0978.

CHAPTER 10

1. Mathew Rodriguez, "CPAC Speaker Michael Knowles Says 'Transgenderism Must Be Eradicated,'" *Them*, March 6, 2023, https://www.them.us/story/michael-knowles-transgenderism-cpac.

2. Madison Pauly, "Inside the Secret Working Group That Helped Push Anti-Trans Laws across the Country," *Mother Jones*, March 8, 2023, https://www.mother jones.com/politics/2023/03/anti-trans-transgender-health-care-ban-legislation-bill-minors-children-lgbtq/.

3. Sky News Australia, "Cancel Culture Comes for Mum and Dad," *Paul Murray Live*, April 12, 2021, https://www.youtube.com/watch?v=kzjv0fIvtHk.

4. Laura Garcia, "A Guide to Prebunking: A Promising Way to Inoculate against Misinformation," First Draft, September 2, 2022, https://firstdraftnews.org/articles/a-guide-to-prebunking-a-promising-way-to-inoculate-against-misinformation/.

5. Claire Robertson et al., "Negativity Drives Online News Consumption," *Nature Human Behaviour* 7, no. 5 (March 16, 2023): 812–22, https://doi.org/10.1038/s41562-023-01538-4.

CHAPTER 12

1. David Oliver, "'Being Transgender Is Not a Medical Condition': The Meaning of Trans Broken Arm Syndrome," *USA Today*, March 31, 2022, https://www.usatoday.com/story/life/health-wellness/2021/07/27/trans-broken-arm-syndrome-what-it-how-combat-discrimination-health-care/8042475002/.

BIBLIOGRAPHY

Baker, Kellan E., Lisa M Wilson, Ritu Sharma, Vadim Dukhanin, Kristen McArthur, and Karen A Robinson. "Hormone Therapy, Mental Health, and Quality of Life among Transgender People: A Systematic Review." *Journal of the Endocrine Society* 5, no. 4 (2021). https://doi.org/10.1210/jendso/bvab011.

Garcia, Laura. "A Guide to Prebunking: A Promising Way to Inoculate against Misinformation." First Draft, September 2, 2022. https://firstdraftnews.org/articles/a-guide-to-prebunking-a-promising-way-to-inoculate-against-misinformation/.

Heiden Rootes, Katie M., Christi R. Mcgeorge, Joanne Salas, and Samantha Levine. "The Effects of Gender Identity Change Efforts on Black, Latinx, and White Transgender and Gender Nonbinary Adults: Implications for Ethical Clinical Practice." *Journal of Marital and Family Therapy* 48, no. 3 (2021). http://dx.doi.org/10.1111/jmft.12575.

Lavery, Daniel M. *Something That May Shock and Discredit You*. New York: Atria Books, 2020.

Minnesota Department of Health. "Summary of Findings: A Review of Scientific Evidence of Conversion Therapy." April 11, 2022. https://www.health.state.mn.us/people/conversiontherapy.pdf.

Morton, M. H., A. Dworsky, and G. M. Samuels. "Missed Opportunities: Youth Homelessness in America. National Estimates." Voices of Youth Count, 2017. https://voicesofyouthcount.org/brief/national-estimates-of-youth-homelessness/.

Oliver, David. "'Being Transgender Is Not a Medical Condition': The Meaning of Trans Broken Arm Syndrome." *USA Today*, March 31, 2022. https://www.usa

today.com/story/life/health-wellness/2021/07/27/trans-broken-arm-syndrome
-what-it-how-combat-discrimination-health-care/8042475002/.

Pauly, Madison. "Inside the Secret Working Group That Helped Push Anti-Trans
Laws across the Country." *Mother Jones*, March 8, 2023. https://www.mother
jones.com/politics/2023/03/anti-trans-transgender-health-care-ban-legislation
-bill-minors-children-lgbtq/.

Reed, Erin. "US Internal Refugee Crisis: 130–260k Trans People Have Already
Fled." *Erin in the Morning*, June 13, 2023. https://www.erininthemorning.com
/p/us-internal-refugee-crisis-130-260k.

Reyes, Yacob. "Transition-Related Surgery Limited to Teens, Not 'Young Kids.'
Even Then, It's Rare." PolitiFact, August 10, 2022. https://www.politifact.com
/factchecks/2022/aug/10/ron-desantis/transition-related-surgery-limited-teens
-not-young/.

Robertson, Claire, Nicolas Pröllochs, Kaoru Schwarzenegger, Philip Pärnamets,
Clara Pretus, and Stefan Feuerriegel. "Negativity Drives Online News Consumption." *Nature Human Behaviour* 7, no. 5 (March 16, 2023): 812–22. https://doi.
org/10.1038/s41562-023-01538-4.

Rodriguez, Mathew. "CPAC Speaker Michael Knowles Says 'Transgenderism Must
Be Eradicated.'" *Them*, March 6, 2023. https://www.them.us/story/michael
-knowles-transgenderism-cpac.

Schillace, Brandy. "The Forgotten History of the World's First Trans Clinic."
Scientific American, May 10, 2021. https://www.scientificamerican.com/article
/the-forgotten-history-of-the-worlds-first-trans-clinic/.

Silk, Susan, and Barry Goldman. "Ring Theory: How Not to Say the Wrong Thing."
Los Angeles Times, May 12, 2020. https://www.latimes.com/opinion/op-ed
/la-xpm-2013-apr-07-la-oe-0407-silk-ring-theory-20130407-story.html.

Sky News Australia. "Cancel Culture Comes for Mum and Dad." *Paul Murray Live*,
April 12, 2021. https://www.youtube.com/watch?v=kzjv0flvtHk.

Strong Family Alliance. "Faith-Based Organizations." November 9, 2022. https://
www.strongfamilyalliance.org/hopeful-voices/faith-based-organizations/.

Tanner, Lindsey. "How Common Is Transgender Treatment Regret, Detransitioning?" AP News, August 18, 2023. https://apnews.com/article/transgender-treat
ment-regret-detransition-371e927ec6e7a24cd9c77b5371c6ba2b.

Tordoff, Diana M., Jonathon William Wanta, Arin Collin, Cesalie Stepney, David J.
Inwards-Breland, and Kym R. Ahrens. "Mental Health Outcomes in Transgender
and Nonbinary Youths Receiving Gender-Affirming Care." *JAMA* 5, no. 2 (February 25, 2022): e220978. https://doi.org/10.1001/jamanetworkopen.2022.0978.

Turban, Jack L., Stephanie Loo, Anthony N. Almazan, and Alex S. Keuroghlian.
"Factors Leading to 'Detransition' among Transgender and Gender Diverse

People in the United States: A Mixed-Methods Analysis." *LGBT Health* 8, no. 4 (June 1, 2021): 273–80. https://doi.org/10.1089/lgbt.2020.0437.

Valentine, Sarah E., and Jillian C. Shipherd. "A Systematic Review of Social Stress and Mental Health among Transgender and Gender Non-Conforming People in the United States." *Clinical Psychology Review* 66 (December 1, 2018): 24–38. https://doi.org/10.1016/j.cpr.2018.03.003.

UCSF Gender Affirming Health Program. "Welcome." https://transcare.ucsf.edu /welcome-0.

ACKNOWLEDGMENTS

The number of people who have lifted me up over the course of my life is nothing short of miraculous. Because of the nature of my work, of this book, of my career, and of who I am as a person, the creation of this book is possible only because of the people who chose to be champions for me at every stage of my journey.

I didn't set out to be a public speaker, but after the amazing team at TEDx Brandeis helped me share my story with the world, I realized I had an opportunity to make a difference far bigger than one talk. Brian, Jamie, and Dave, you saw what I had the potential to be far sooner than I did, but you believed in me enough for all of us. To you, and countless others who spoke my name in rooms where I wasn't to ask how I could get there, thank you so much.

To Jenn, for extending the offer to me to join an incredible PYP writer's group when this book was barely more than a spark, thank you for having the tools, the brilliance, and the community to fan the flames of this passion project. To Heather, this project would not exist at all without you. You saw what this book had the chance to be, and with infinite patience and wisdom helped me shape it into what it is now. Thank you for believing in me. To my incredible agent, Jessica, thank you for never giving up on this book, patiently answering my many panicked emails, and being an extremely wise guide through this process. To everyone behind the scenes at Bookends as well, thank you so much for putting your hearts into this book.

ACKNOWLEDGMENTS

Thank you to the whole crew at Left Bank Books who showed me the magic of queer authors and celebrated the milestones of this book with me at every turn. Thank you to the countless coffee shops and libraries where this book was born and raised.

I had so many friends who helped me get this book across the finish line. Friends who sat with me in cars and at dinner tables letting me dream as big as I could about what this book could be, friends who commiserated with me about the woes of the publishing process, friends who volunteered to edit early chapters for free. (You tried to warn me about my run-on sentences, but here we are.) To my people, not just the ones who worked directly with me on this book, but all of you: thank you for calling, for waiting patiently for my texts back, for playing games and taking walks and finding all manner of ways to keep me sane these past few years.

To J, to become boys and then men together has been one of the great honors of my life. Thank you for getting me here. Liam, thank you for teaching me how to find my own form of masculinity and celebrate it, and for teaching me all the secret codes of male friendships so I could seem cooler. It almost worked!

To the community organizations here in St. Louis that have shown me what it means to fight with everything you have, to the organizations who have shown me what it looks like to heal ourselves and each other, thank you. The way we have showed up for each other fills me with so much hope. Reader, if you're still here and have the means to do so, toss a few dollars to any of these incredible groups of champions: Metro Trans Umbrella Group (MTUG), PFLAG, TransParent USA, PROMO, SQSH, and Triangle Wellness Collective.

To parents and families of trans youth, y'all are some of the fiercest advocates I know. Knowing that there are enough of you that this book was worth writing—and worth selling—keeps me going. Thank you for fighting for us. Beth and Susan, you are two of the fiercest advocates I've ever met. To every parent who has ever reached out to me wanting to know how to stand up for their VIP, thank you for trusting me, for showing me all the ways a parent could speak the language of love, and for pouring support into this community.

To my brothers, sisters, and siblings in the trans community, you are why I do what I do. I have had the distinct honor of meeting and learning from so many brilliant trans people. I have learned about life, love, organizing, resilience, and so much from you all. Bryce and Michaela, you have been both personal and professional role models, confidants, teammates, and cheerleaders for so much of my journey. I have learned so much from you. To all of the trans people in my life, your magic, joy, and community is healing to me, and I learn from you all every single day. To every trans man with a defiantly graying beard, to every trans kid with a defiantly brilliant smile, just knowing you're out there keeps me going. Thank you.

To the family I had the miraculous fortune of being born into, thank you. You met me with love, you built a home where I knew I was seen as I was, and I will always be eternally grateful for that. Dad, you showed me exactly the type of man I want to be. Mom, you somehow manage both to keep me grounded in reality and help me build out my wildest ideas into real-life plans. To both of you, we built this plane together while we flew it, and I'm thankful for the amount of research, patience, and love you put into learning how to show up for me. Hannah and Shea, in addition to being the funniest people I have ever met, you have been such passionate advocates for me since the day I came out. I am so grateful to have you both on my team.

To my whole family, you all chose to welcome me as I was with open arms, and it means so much to me to know that you have been cheering me on and loving me through every step of this journey.

To the family that I am building, thank you. Oliver, despite my best efforts, you remain illiterate. I will thank you anyway because you are the best dog ever. Samantha, by the time you read this you'll be my wife, and I am so, so happy that we get to choose each other every day. You have believed in this book, celebrated the good ideas, listened patiently through the terrible ideas, and held my hand through the moments of fear and doubt since its conception in 2019. I am so honored to grow by your side and cannot wait to see the power couple that we continue to grow into.

Finally, to you, reader: The better world we're dreaming of feels a little closer knowing you're on our team.

INDEX

ABOUT THE AUTHOR

Ben V. Greene currently lives in St. Louis, Missouri, with his wife, Samantha, and his dog, Oliver. In 2019 at Brandeis University, he delivered the TEDx Talk "Where Are You Sitting?" on transgender inclusion and allyship, which launched his career as an international public speaker. He is a fierce advocate for the trans community and has devoted his work to spreading empathy, education, and storytelling about the trans experience. He is passionate about educating people from a place of heartfelt welcoming—no matter where they're starting from.